C. N. Righter

THE BIBLE IN THE LEVANT;

OR THE

LIFE AND LETTERS OF THE

REV. C. N. RIGHTER,

AGENT OF THE AMERICAN BIBLE SOCIETY IN THE LEVANT.

BY SAMUEL IRENÆUS PRIME.

NEW YORK:
SHELDON & COMPANY.
BOSTON: GOULD & LINCOLN.
1859.

Entered, according to Act of Congress, in the year 1859, by
SHELDON & CO.,
In the Clerk's Office of the District Court of the United States for the Southern District of New York.

DEDICATION.

TO THE MOTHER

WHO FREELY GAVE HER BELOVED SON

TO THE SERVICE OF GOD IN A FOREIGN LAND

AND DID NOT REGRET THE GIFT WHEN HE DIED FAR AWAY,

This Book is Respectfully Inscribed,

PREFACE.

Few words of preface are required for this unpretending volume.

A man's life is not to be measured by the number of his years. It has been well said that some die old at thirty and others young at fourscore. The subject of this sketch was formed for high accomplishment, and to all human appearances was destined to do a great work in the service to which he was called. His early removal was a sad blow to the host of friends who were looking to his future with high hopes. But the thoughts of Infinite wisdom are higher than ours. And while we bow with resignation to the will of Him who called our friend and brother so early to himself, we find a mournful satisfaction in preparing these memorials of one whose name and virtues will long be fragrant in the hearts of all who knew him.

CONTENTS.

—o—

CHESTER N. RIGHTER.

CHAPTER I.

THE AUTHOR'S FIRST MEETING WITH RIGHTER—GENERAL CHARACTER—STRIKING FEATURES—A SEA VOYAGE WITH HIM.

SIX years ago, in the spring of 1853, the writer of these pages, a poor invalid, was lying on a pile of trunks at the end of a pier in the East River, waiting, with many others, for the steam tug that was to take him and them to a ship in the stream. Worn out with long protracted sickness, embarking without a single companion for a year of foreign travel, he was sadly despondent and half inclined to abandon the voyage. At this moment two young men were introduced to him; both of them ministers of the gospel, both of them just about to embark for foreign travel, both of them intending to make the tour of Europe, and to journey into the East. One of these gentlemen was the Rev. George E. Hill, of Boston, the other was Chester Newell Righter, the subject of this sketch. A mutual sympathy seemed instantaneously to unite us. In a few moments the plans of the year were compared, and without any further concert or agreement, it fell out that we joined our fortunes, and together made the journey, with scarcely any separations till we returned home, in the same vessel, in the spring of 1854.

Righter was a genial, warm-hearted, noble young man. A good scholar, a fluent speaker, ready in conversation, full of ardor, enthusiasm and energy, buoyant and hopeful, never doubting or afraid, never sick or weary, with exuberant spirits and inexhaustible powers of enjoying or suffering, he was just the companion one wants on land or sea, in desert or city, by night or day.

His eyes had failed while he was pursuing his studies for the sacred ministry, and he had been wisely counselled to spend a year in relaxation and travel. On shipboard the fine points of his character were soon developed. A week at sea brings out the weaknesses as well as the strength of men. He was with me in all weathers, and in various lands and seas, in times to try the patience, and the faith, and every virtue of the soul; and during all the time he was with me, I never knew him to be other than a high-minded, honorable, faithful, Christian gentleman and friend.

When others were sea-sick, when every passenger on the steamer was stretched out in helpless distress, victims of that malady which everybody, except the victim, laughs *at*, but *to* which almost every one succumbs, Righter would stride the deck, swinging his arms and rejoicing in the storm—fearless of danger, and strong in his exemption from the falling sickness to which all around him were a prey. This was a fair type and exhibition of his character. What was to be done, he was ready to do; what was to be borne, he was ready to suffer. Prompt in his decisions, tenacious of his purposes, self-sacrificing and obliging, when the feelings of others were involved, he was the first in every movement to promote the general comfort of the company, the last to yield when difficulties were to be overcome.

His principles of right and wrong were intelligently settled, and he had no occasion to be "making up his mind" as to the path of duty. The way was always plain, and he pressed straight forward in the fear of God, and without any fear of man. *Religion* was a well-spring of life and joy in his soul. In all places and times he was the same earnest, outspoken, uniform Christian; never obtruding his opinions on those to whom they were not due, but never ashamed, afraid, or unable to give a reason for the hope that was in him. Yet he was modest with all his self-reliance, gentle with iron firmness, easily to be entreated, while he was bold as a lion.

With such a rare and beautiful mingling of elements in his character, I marked him out as a man who had a work to do for his age and the world. Often we lay on deck as we were traversing from land to land the Mediterranean Sea, and when the stars were looking down on us we would while away the hours with long and wandering talks of the future, and then I found that the aspirations of his soul were in harmony with my hopes and prophecies of his career. He was burning to *be* what I was sure he *would* be, if God had work for him on this earth. No matter what it was, if the mountains were to be brought down, or the wilderness to be reclaimed by human agency, he was ready to do what the Lord would have him do. And more; he was anxious to be at work. I do not know that the fires of an earth-born, selfish ambition, a paltry spirit of self-glory, ever burned for a moment in his manly breast. He must have been ambitious—it was part of his nature. But it was a noble, baptized, holy ambition, to do something for God and mankind. He longed to see the world, to know it, to take the measure of it, to compass its wants, to study the ways and means to meet them, and, with a full consciousness of his own inherent physical and mental adaptedness to labor, he was willing to give himself as a servant, a soldier, a follower, or a leader, to be used as the Lord should appoint in the field of the world.

This was the man with whom I became acquainted under circumstances of peculiar interest, and in a few days, from a stranger, he became a friend and brother beloved. He grew close to my heart. He was with me in times of trial and peril; in seasons of rich enjoyment; the wonders and glories of nature and art, in the course of a year's travel in Europe and the East, were shared together, and when he went out again into the foreign field to do a mighty work, and there died in the midst of his labors, I mourned his death as that of a brother, and cried with David over Jonathan, "I am distressed for thee, my brother: very pleasant hast thou been unto me, thy love to me was wonderful."

And this tribute to his memory is but a feeble memorial of one of the purest, noblest young men it was ever my joy to know.

CHAPTER II.

PARENTAGE, BIRTH, AND EARLY EDUCATION—CONVERSION AND RELIGIOUS EXERCISES—REVIVAL IN SCHOOL.

He was born September 25, 1824, at Parsippany, in New Jersey. His estimable parents were among the most respectable people in the rich agricultural region of Morris County. His mother was eminently a devout woman, full of faith and prayer, and consecrating her children with all the ardor of a mother's love and the confidence of a firm belief in the promises, to the service of God.

All the children—there were two daughters and four sons—had the best opportunities of early education, and one of the sons studied a profession, and is a successful lawyer in the city of Newark, N. J.

Chester, in very early life, disclosed a fondness for books. Apt to learn, and ambitious of excelling, he made rapid attainments in learning. At the age of twelve he was sent from home to a classical school at Wantage, N. J., under the care of his uncle, Mr. E. A. Stiles, where he pursued his studies with great success, and was fitted for college. One of his cousins, who was in the same family, has furnished me with a sketch of the character and progress of *the boy*, and it is so like *the man* that I must copy the portrait here: "Even then, when he was only twelve years old, were largely developed that fearless assurance and determined purpose which distinguished him in after life, and formed him for action in so wide a field. After a few months' study here, the school was suspended; Chester returned home and remained there two years and a half, and when his uncle, Mr. Stiles, resumed his school again at Wantage, Chester joined him, and remained under his instruction until he was prepared to enter college.

"During the second year of this period of study, a series of religious meetings was held in the Clove Church, about a mile from the school, by the Rev. T. S. Ward. The pupils were allowed to attend the services, or to stay at home, as they preferred. Righter was one of the few who attended them from the beginning regularly. The interest in the meetings increased. On the third evening all the teachers and pupils attended. The house was thronged, and the audience deeply solemn under the preaching of the word. Many were powerfully impressed by the truth and the Spirit. The next morning young Righter went to his uncle with the great question 'What must I do to be saved?' That night on retiring to his room, he found his brother, who was a teacher in the school, sitting at his table writing, and he exclaimed, 'O brother, how can you sit still and write while I am perishing in my sins?' His brother invited him to repent of his sins and turn to Christ with all his heart. He bade him kneel with him and give himself up to the Lord Jesus Christ for time and eternity. They knelt, and prayed together; wrestled long and earnestly on their knees, till the awakened, anxious, convicted sinner submitted to God. Light broke in upon his soul. Peace was shed abroad in his heart. He arose a new creature in Christ Jesus.

"The next morning as he entered the parlor where family worship was to be held, his countenance reflected the calmness and joy of his soul. His teacher and uncle said to him at once:

"'Chester, I trust you have found the Saviour.'

"'Yes, uncle,' he replied, 'I have given myself away to be his for ever.'

"The interest of the whole school in the subject of religion was so great, it was thought best to suspend the usual studies and hold a prayer meeting in the parlor during the forenoon. Nearly all the pupils attended. Young Righter was called on to offer the first prayer. A mere boy of sixteen, in the midst of his companions, it might have been feared that he would hesitate when thus suddenly summoned to stand up as a *Christian.* But he was ready. With equal modesty and decision he rose and began with humble confession of sin, grateful acknowledgment of his joy and gratitude on account of sins forgiven, and then he prayed that all his associates might come to Christ without delay and share in the blessings of salvation. His words were fluent, for he had ready command of language, and his prayer was heard with deep emotions by his companions, and, we may believe, in heaven also, for the work of grace went on and others were brought in. With them he organized a prayer meeting, which was held *daily, at noon,* behind a haystack, in the midst of the winter season. If the daily noon prayer meetings were held earlier than this, I have not seen any account of them. These boys kept them up, with great interest, regardless of the weather; their young hearts being warm and their petitions earnest for more and more of the Holy Spirit. This was the beginning of our friend's Christian life. In March of the same year, 1841, with thirty others, he made a public profession of religion, uniting with 'the Clove' church, in that neighborhood. Now he was a professed follower of Christ, a soldier of the cross, young but strong in the Lord. His face was set toward heaven, and so was his heart.

"Grace begun in his soul wrought a great and decided change. With the resolute will and energy, which I have mentioned, he had also an irritable temper, and these traits of character made him often overbearing. He had been the leader in the sports of the school, and many had found him too fond of having his own way. But it is the testimony of those who knew him then, that from the time he became a child of God, he was indeed a new creature. Patient perseverance took the place of fitful haste, decision in the right succeeded to a desire to have things to suit himself. Moral courage was soon revealed in his unbending opposition to all that was wrong in the school, even when he was compelled to stand alone. His example was thus a powerful aid in the discipline of the school, and his influence was felt in-doors and out, upon all who were with him. The secret of this great change, and the rapid progress of grace in his soul, was his invariable habit of prayer. Without ostentation, he led a life of constant communion with God; seeking, day by day, the help he needed to overcome indwelling sin, get the victory over himself, and to be qualified for the service of the Saviour.

"During a school vacation, he was at home. His father was not a professor of religion, but Chester was encouraged to conduct family worship, which he did with readiness. One morning he had made arrangements with a friend for an excursion that required them to make an early start. The horses were at the door. His friend was impatient, and reminded him that his hurry seemed to be over, asking him why he delayed. Righter simply remarked that the family were not quite ready for prayers, and he would start as soon as they had had morning worship. This friend was a neglecter of religion, and never had been in the habit of attending 'family prayers,' but without saying a word, he took his seat and remained, apparently interested in the service.

"Such an incident serves to show the early decision which Righter had made to be prompt and faithful in the performance of Christian duty, and the *habit* thus formed grew with him till it became a part of his sanctified nature, an abiding principle which governed him at home and abroad, on land and sea. He was a praying youth and a praying man. He obtained strength in prayer. Great trials and strong conflicts were before him. Few men have been so soon called to make such sacrifices as he made and to endure such temptations, and if he had not been strong with God, the world and the flesh would have prevailed. Then this record had never been made."

CHAPTER III.

CHOOSING A PROFESSION—STRUGGLES AND DECISION—COLLEGE—THEOLOGICAL SEMINARY—LETTER FROM REV. GEORGE E. HILL—FIRST PREACHING.

RIGHTER was now at a point in his history where the choice of a profession or pursuit must be made. In the ardor of his first love for Christ and his cause, we would expect him to look at the ministry as his field, and that he would throw himself, heart and soul, into the work of preparation for that high and holy calling. Why should he not?

There were two reasons, at least, that he must meet and answer before he could decide the question that now pressed itself home on his conscience.

He was naturally of a jovial disposition. Fond of fun and frolic when a boy, he did not lose his love for innocent amusements when he forsook all that he knew were sinful. This was now in his way when he thought of entering the hallowed walks of the ministry. His fondness for pleasantry might degenerate into levity. Certainly he was now far from having that sobriety of manner which befits the clerical profession. If he should become a minister, and then dishonor the name and office, by his inconsistent deportment, to the injury of the cause and the ruin of souls, it were better that he had never been born, or that he had turned the current of his life into some channel where his example would be less conspicuous, and so less injurious. But this was not a fatal objection. He had found, by his own experience in the divine life, that grace could overcome nature, and his own good sense assured him that cheerfulness was far more desirable than austerity in the minister of the gospel. He was willing to trust God for help to subdue all that was positively wrong. While he would be a joyful Christian, he did not wish to appear to be anything else. This objection was, therefore, laid aside, but there was one more serious.

The father of Righter, if a Christian, was reserved in regard to his feelings, and made no profession, even to his nearest friends, of being interested, personally, in religion. Possessed of an ample property, and being largely engaged in business, he was a man of the world. Safe in his judgments, but enterprising and successful, he had several distinct branches of business, agricultural, mercantile, and manufacturing, in which he was engaged, with the aid of his sons. It was against his wishes that his son, Chester, began to turn his thoughts toward the ministry. It would be far more to the father's taste if the son would enter into business with him. It was easy for Mr. Righter to set before his son inducements of a worldly nature, that would compel him to pause, and think twice and long, before he threw them aside, as unworthy of his pursuit and love. Righter has told me that this was a temptation and trial. While he justly regarded the gospel ministry as the wide field for usefulness that he burned to enter, he was not ignorant that he must sacrifice the prospect of wealth and future ease. But the trial was greater when he saw his father advancing in years, and earnestly anxious to secure him in such pursuits as would make his son the companion and comfort of his old age. To become a minister he must leave houses and lands, father and mother, for Christ's sake. This was the alternative. He has assured me that he was able without much of a struggle to forego the attractions of the world, but he desired greatly to please his father, and his mind was long in the balances of doubt as to what was duty in these circumstances. But the Lord was calling him, and the call proved to be irresistible. To his young and buoyant spirit no pleasure on earth was more alluring than the joy of publishing glad tidings of salvation. No wealth was more precious in his sight than the unsearchable riches of Christ, which one who called himself less than the least of all saints was permitted to preach to perishing men. And when he saw in the gospel that, in this very connexion, he was told by his Master to leave father and mother for the sake of the work to which he was called, he resolved in the dew of his youth, to give himself to the ministry of reconciliation.

With this purpose once formed, he went forward steadily to realize the desires of his soul.

In the fall of 1842 he entered Yale College, and after completing his course of study there and graduating with honor, he pursued the study of theology at New Haven and Andover. One of his classmates in College, who was afterwards an intimate friend, and our companion in travel, the Rev. George E. Hill, has given me a few memoranda of his literary career which I here employ.

"He entered college with high resolutions to lead a life of devotion to study, and to such discipline of heart as would prepare him for the profession which he sought. He was regarded by his associates as exceedingly reserved and diffident. His reputation was that of a diligent student, rather than a social companion, and rarely did he mingle in the sports of college life.

With his fine talents and this exemplary diligence, it was a matter of course that his standing as a scholar was high. Modest and retiring, but always a gentleman in his bearing and address, he was universally respected and esteemed. Indeed I never knew that he had an enemy.

"We were together again in the closing year of our theological studies, and then for the first time I began really to know the value of our friend. He was still the same diligent student, but his soul was now glowing with a warm ambition to be useful in the service of Christ. His former reserve had melted away. He was ready to speak for his Master, and earnestly engaged in winning souls for him. This strong desire was seen and felt in his labors in a Bible Class connected with the Centre Church, New Haven.

"I well remember too, the ardor with which he entered upon our first preaching enterprise, in the little brick school-house at Hampden, five miles east of the city. Here we held religious service every Sabbath evening, in the winter's cold, but we were warm for our hearts burned within us, as we walked by the way. It was then and there, in speaking for the first time as an ambassador of Christ to his fellow-men, that his tongue was really loosed, and his whole soul glowed in his earnest face as he besought men to be reconciled to God. How often on the vessel's deck, and in strange lands beyond the sea, as we have sung together those familiar songs of Zion, has he spoken of the meetings in the brick school-house, as among the happiest memories of his student life.

"Of the subsequent character and career of our friend and brother I have no need to write to you, for you knew him afterward, even better than I. But his uniform benevolence, his *un*-selfishness, his tender regard for the interests and the feelings of others; his unaffected modesty, coupled with a manly heroism that despised danger and never felt fear; his fervent and consistent piety; his powers of endurance and his willingness to do and to suffer in the service of his Master, all this and more you know, and will portray, if you put your pen to the delightful work of perpetuating the memory of our beloved Righter."

CHAPTER IV.

HINDRANCES—FAILURE OF HIS EYES—GOES ABROAD—CROSSES THE OCEAN—FIRST IMPRESSIONS OF ENGLAND—THE CONTINENT.

DURING the latter part of his course of theological study, Righter was afflicted with weakness of his eyes. The usual remedies were resorted to, and temporary repose was tried without benefit. He was advised to spend a year or two in foreign travel, that entire cessation from study for such a length of time might give his eyes a fair opportunity to recuperate. Such a prescription was not disagreeable to the patient. It fell in with his own predilections, and finding in his friend Hill, whose letter has just been given, a congenial companion, he made arrangements at once for a journey into foreign lands.

His journals during this tour were kept with great regularity, and a *daily* record is made of every event of interest that occurred, every place that he visited, every object that he studied, every notable person that he met. But these records are the briefest possible—often mere catchwords; for the use of his eyes, even to make the entries in his diary, was a trial to which he was afraid to subject them. He designed, if it were right for him to do so, to correspond with some newspaper while he was abroad, but after a few attempts at writing he was obliged to desist, and confine himself to short notes in his journals, and occasional letters to his friends. These manuscript records of travel, going over the same ground that I traversed with him, are now lying around me, and they awaken a thousand pleasing recollections, as I turn over the pages and find my own name so often among the incidents of that varied year. His parting with his parents at the wharf, with other friends who went with us down the bay, his feelings in view of the separation and hopes of the future are hinted at in terms that are easily intelligible to the eye of affection, and disclose the warmth of his love. The voyage is to him a succession of joyous days and charming nights. In the morning he is getting up athletic sports for exercise: in the afternoon he is reading or talking French with the ladies: in the evening some literary exercise is on hand for the entertainment of the passengers. Sabbath comes, and he is holding religious meetings with the seamen. Others are stricken down with sea-sickness, and I find that he mentions me as the first victim, while he flatters himself that he will escape altogether. He does not. A slight attack knocks him over, and teaches him that he is not more than human. But he was speedily on his feet again, and that was the last of his maritime disasters. All the way over the sea he was rejoicing in the beauty, the grandeur, and glory of the ocean. In the storms he was confident, and delighted to fix himself in the bows of the ship that he might see and feel the power and majesty of the waves. And if he had been compelled to say with the Psalmist, "All thy billows have gone over me," I think he would have been calm and trusting, for he knew that in the uttermost part of the sea the hand of the Lord would lead and uphold him. He was not anxious to reach the shores of Europe. Our voyage in a packet-ship, Capt. Hovey, with a pleasant cabinful of passengers, was made in sixteen days, and Righter was one of many who would have been glad to extend it a week longer.

On landing at Portsmouth, on Sabbath morning, he walked to the Parish Church of St. Thomas, where we united in thanksgiving to Almighty God for his care over us while on the deep. The next day he was wandering over the Isle of Wight. At Ryde he calls on the Rev. Dr. Ferguson with whom he is greatly pleased, and the gratification would seem to have been mutual, for he acknowledges the gift of a volume of sermons from the Dr. as a token of his regard. He admires the lovely scenery through which he passes; the smooth roads, the hedges and flowers, and green fields, a vision of rural culture and widespread taste in the order of nature, which he had never enjoyed before. The ancient Carisbrooke Castle impresses him deeply with its walls and battlements, its remarkable well, its romantic history. But even more does his spirit find refreshment and delight in a pilgrimage to the grave of the Dairyman's Daughter in Areton Church-yard. He notes the tolling of the bell and the funeral procession that marked his visit there. He gathers flowers from among the tombs to send to friends at home; for his heart was with them always, and when enjoying things abroad the most, he was always thinking of ways and means to share it with those far away.

He hastens to London and records his "first impressions" of the great city. Lost in its vastness, he seems, from his brief notes, to be overwhelmed with a sense of the extent and power of the great metropolis, so that it required time to adjust his mind to the new world by which he was surrounded. But he was soon studying it systematically and thoroughly, visiting its great benevolent institutions, finding access to public men, enjoying the private hospitalities of many kind friends whom he found or made.

He pursued his journey to France and Switzerland, ENJOYING everything with a heartiness refreshing to his companions, and making notes in his journal, giving glimpses of his own character that will present him pleasingly to the reader. We will make a few extracts from his note books which are before us, to the number of a dozen or more.

CHAPTER V.

EXTRACTS FROM HIS JOURNALS—PARIS—MEETINGS WITH CHRISTIAN FRIENDS—SWITZERLAND—CHAMOUNI AND THE ALPS.

FROM MR. RIGHTER'S JOURNAL.

SUNDAY, June 10th, 1853.—In the afternoon we receive an invitation to attend a little prayer meeting of Americans at the house of a good lady resident here, and we hail the opportunity with joy; we go, and find a delightful little gathering and union of Christian hearts there, and it indeed seems like the house of God and the gate of heaven to our souls. It is proposed, as the need is peculiarly felt by those present, to make an effort to establish an American Church in Paris, where service will be performed for their benefit especially; which shall be attractive to them, and will make them feel at home in their church in a strange land. It meets the approbation and earnest prayer of all present, and I trust may result through the effort and prayer of that little meeting in Rue d'Astorq. In the evening we hear Mr. Bridel in his neat little evangelical chapel. The tones of his voice are very touching, and much effect is produced on the audience. The singing in French, by the congregation, is very delightful indeed to us who have been so long from heart-felt devotional worship.

MONDAY, June 11th.—In the evening we attend another meeting to consult in reference to the expediency of establishing an American Church in Paris. The need is felt deeply by all present. Rev. Mr. Bridel, the protestant evangelical French minister in the city, gives an affecting account of the cases in which young men from America, entire strangers, have written to him in times of sickness, to come and visit them. And how far more grateful and useful to them in such cases, would be an American Christian brother from their own native land. He would be the medium, also, between the Americans and French, the religious ambassador here. There are two hundred American families resident here, and five hundred or two thousand persons constantly here for business or pleasure. All these might be attracted to a house of God. I trust the movement will meet with a cordial response from America.

WEDNESDAY, July 27th, 1853.—At length we arrive in the lovely vale of Chamouni with the summit of Mont Blanc before us, and the *mer de glace* and mountain peaks around. It is a lovely spot in a clear summer evening, as the last rays of the setting sun are lingering on the monarch of mountains rolled in clouds with a diadem of snow circling his brow.

In the evening we go out to take a view around from the church steps near by, and here we fully realize the poetry, and yet the truthfulness of Coleridge's hymn written at Chamouni. The air is clear and cloudless now, a light is shining midway up the mountain; the fire of a party who are making the ascent, and have encamped there for the night, and Jupiter, bright and beautiful, is shining just above the summit. It is indeed a most sublime view. We gaze and admire for a time, then return to our hotel, engage our guides and mules, and make all our arrangements for the ascent of the Jardin on the morrow.

THURSDAY, July 28th.—The morning breaks bright and clear. We rise at six and mount our mules provided with guides, provisions, thick shoes, Alpine stock, green vails, spectacles, and thick coats, for the journey to the Jardin. We cross the green meadow, the Arve, and ascend the mountain side. A party of ladies are before us winding their way up the mountain side, a picturesque view. We soon overtake and pass them. Then we have a party above, and these far below, in connexion with the valley beneath, the green mountains far above, the lofty range on the opposite side, the silver-threaded cascade winding adown it, the *mer de glace*, the swift running Arveiron at its base, all form a panoramic view, the most sublime and beautiful. We cross frequent Alpine torrents and pass fountains gushing from the mountain side. At one a company of Swiss girls tempt us with water and refreshments for sale. We take a hasty draught, and mount up, until at length in three hours we reach the Montanvert, the best point for viewing the *mer de glace*, and the surrounding scenery. Here we take a little wine, leave our trusty mules, and commence the ascent to the Jardin on foot. We pass along the steep mountain side, clinging with our hands and pointing our pike, where a single slip would precipitate us hundreds of feet into the chasm below. Yet so great is our excitement and courage for the moment, and, moreover, so faithful are our guides that we have not the least sense of danger. Now we reach the *mer de glace*, a sea of frozen waves, with deep crevasses and gorges, worn by the melting snow, and waterfalls rushing down the mountain side. This seems, indeed, frightful, accompanied with the roar of the water far below, the fall of the rocks, and the avalanches from the peaks on either side. Yet we advance, leaping the chasms, and guarding against the covert pitfalls till we have crossed a portion of this frozen sea and reached an intermediate point of rocks and stones, borne down by the winter's avalanche. We look back and are amazed at the dangers we have passed, yet, there are still more before us. The view is now grand indeed; the summits around are covered with snow; numbers shoot up far into the sky of solid rock—massive, and of purple hue, while one just before us, is clad with green grass and blooming flowers. We strengthen ourselves by a draught of cool ice-water, and advance over a still more dangerous path, till we reach the base of this peak, two hundred feet high. Here the sun shines in the rarified air with scorching heat. We put on our green veils and spectacles, and begin the toilsome ascent. So bracing and exhilarating has been the air thus far, that we scarcely feel fatigued; but we have now passed from winter to midsummer heat, and begin to feel quite exhausted, and we sit down here among the violets and Alpine roses, and refresh ourselves with the beautiful view of summer and winter, side by side, and rocky snow-capped grandeur all around—perhaps the most impressive of all, the sea of glaring ice spread out in front. We toil up this steep ascent, cross another belt of snow and ice, and at length, reach the Jardin—a beautiful little oasis of green grass and flowers, amid a desert of rocks and snow around. A stream of cool water gushes from the rocks, and flows through for the refreshment of the weary traveller, and the sun shines here with warmest ray. We find a lady has reached here before us, and is beautifully basking in the sunshine—(where will not enthusiastic woman go?) We pay our compliments to the fair lady, then bestow ourselves on the grass for rest, refreshment, and enjoyment of the scene. How excellent we relish our cold food—ham and wine; but the panoramic scene spread out around must not be lost; we must pluck some flowers, as souvenirs of the place and day, and we cannot remain here but a half hour, yet we have been walking five hours in succession, over snow and ice; clambering rocks and climbing the mountain peaks, and we throw ourselves down upon the rock and enjoy a few moments of refreshing sleep. Now we begin our return—three hours again over the same dangerous path, to Montanvert. The day is clear and almost cloudless, and we enjoy the most perfect view of the sublime scenery, all the way in clear sunlight. Frequent rocks and avalanches are falling and roaring around us, to give effect to all, and we return unharmed, through the guidance and protection of our God, to the mountain where our mules are waiting to take us again to Chamouni. We refresh ourselves again with a cup of milk, and begin the descent. This seems more dangerous than all (though our mules are most trusty), for a single step would plunge us down a steep precipice and dash us to pieces; and the path is steep, jagged, and winding zig-zag down, yet we are so excited with the scene and situation, that we do not fear the danger before us. How beautiful the green valley of grass, and grain, and trees, stretches below, as the sunlight falls upon it; how the last rays of the setting sun play upon yonder summits, till at last they have gone from all save Mont Blanc—still they bathe the monarch's brow with purple and gold, and finally are gone from view. The whole view seems now more picturesque than ever. The water courses of the avalanches above, now clothed with green, the meadow, the silver cascades, the mountain peaks, the *mer de glace*—all in the mellow light of sunset, are surpassingly beautiful.

At length we safely reached our hotel at Cha mouni, after fourteen hours of climbing up and down on foot and on mules—feeling that we had never enjoyed such a day before, and full of gratitude to our God that he has brought us thus happily to its close.

Though the sun has been intensely hot, and the reflection from the ice and snow very great, yet our green vails have protected us almost entirely from sunburn and blister, so frequent and so distressing in such cases—let me recommend it to all. Thus passed a most memorable day of my life, in ascending the Alps to the "Garden of Flowers," and returning to the vale of Chamouni. A refreshing supper, a warm bath, and bathing also the face and feet with cream and brandy, prepared us for a good night's rest.

SATURDAY, 30.—The morning dawns clear, and betokens a fair day for the mountains. We mount our mules at an early hour for Chamouni, a ride of eight hours across a difficult pass. As we pass through the valley we meet peasant girls riding "stride their mules," at full trot, with morning provisions for the village. We choose the most difficult pass of the Col de Balme for the benefit of, by far, the finest views, in a clear day. We mount up the mountain side four hours, passing many cascades, mountain torrents and courses of the winter avalanche by the way; also villages where the peasants live in some sunny spot on the mountain side. Here they cultivate their little patches of grain and potatoes, and grass for themselves and cows, in store for winter, while they drive their cattle far up in summer to pasture. The scene of the herds on the hill-side, and the tinkling of a hundred bells as we pass along, is most delightful. At length we reach the top, where is a comfortable house of refreshment for the traveller. Here the finest view of Mont Blanc and the vale of Chamouni is obtained, and we realize, as never before, the majesty of this monarch of mountains, and still more of Him who made this mount glorious as the sun, clothed him with rainbows, and spread garlands at his feet of loveliest hue. We invert our faces as we have done before, and it changes all into a fancy Alpine scene; we recommend the experiment to all. Here, also, the corleau alone wings his flight above the clouds. But the air blows cold and chilly from Mont Blanc and the snow around, and I dismount my mule, and descend on foot. The scenery is grand and beautiful—of Alpine summits pinnacled in clouds above and below me, and the mule path I am to follow, winding far through the valley. I am above the limit of trees or vegetation, save two months in summer. I pass a little châlet where the shepherds keep their cattle, and make abundance of cheese and butter in the summer months and pass a pleasant word with them. The Swiss peasantry are most sociable and polite to strangers, always bidding you good morning, and giving civil answers to your questions.

I gather flowers as I descend; the number, and variety, and beauty of these Alpine flowers, growing wild upon the mountain side, is almost beyond conception. I find two little kids sleeping in my path; I approach them gently, and caress them, and they return the attention as kindly as if I were their guardian friend. How magnificent the view in this clear full sunlight, amid these crags, and peaks, and flowers, and waterfalls, as I descend alone, in advance of my party, the zigzag path down the mountain. I had experienced such emotions of sublimity, and power, and grandeur, as I have never felt before.

In two hours I reach the base, and rest at a sweet little cottage in the valley, for my friends to overtake me. The family soon gather around me—father, mother, daughters, children and all. I tell them I am from America, and invite them to sing a Swiss song. To this one readily consents, and the music is most beautiful in the open air, and in the magnificence and beauty of nature around me. A little girl brings me flowers, and they set out fresh strawberries, cream, and wine, for my refreshment; and under these circumstances I appreciate and enjoy the view of the valley, cascades, clouds, sky, and mountain grandeur, as I had not done before. How much the presence of human nature, however humble, adds to the beauty of nature herself, however grand.

My friends soon came upon their mules, and I join the party, bidding farewell to the pretty little Swiss demoiselle with twinkling eyes, with whom I had formed a surprisingly romantic glancing acquaintance in so short a time. We ascend two hours, and descend two hours more, amid the most sublime of scenery; viewing the valley of the Rhone, the road of the Simplon, and the vale of Martigny, lying below us; and at six in the evening reach our hotel, quite satisfied with the romance of mule riding, for the present. But this is a low alluvial valley, filled with stagnant water, and infested with malaria and damp; and all the women as well as many of the men, have the goître—a large conical or circular swelling in the throat, six or eight inches in circumference; numbers also have the fever and ague. It is the hotbed of disease; we cannot think of spending the Sabbath here. We take a little refreshment of strawberries and cream, and engage a voiture for the baths of Larey, two hours and a half distant. Little girls meet us at every turn, with flowers, cherries and strawberries for sale; the women and peasants are bringing home upon their heads large bundles of hay and grain from the mountains; they are too poor to keep mules or donkeys, and they carry everything, wood and all, upon their heads, most enormous loads. The air blows damp and pestilential through the valley, yet we must open our carriage windows to see this beautiful cascade, falling hundreds of feet from the solid rock. How splendid is the white dashing spray in the evening light! We ride on, and in one hour reach the baths of Larey; here a worthy host and good hotel receive us for the Sabbath. The evening scenery is beautiful; of a rocky amphitheatre around and a quiet valley below, while the turbid Rhone roars swiftly through. Many ladies appear in front to greet our arrival. It is a French watering-place, and a party of Americans are quite a novelty here. We, however, take a mineral bath and bestow ourselves to bed, much fatigued by the mule and foot mountain travel of the day.

SUNDAY, 31.—The morning breaks again, clear and balmy; it is the Sabbath and our hearts in unison with nature around, join in praise to God for this sweet secluded Sabbath in a vale of Switzerland. The whole scenery around seems in harmony with the day; the sky is more pure, and the clouds float more gently on the Sabbath, and I read my Bible with more spirit and unction than since I left the shores of America. Service is held in French, in the saloon of the hotel. It is evangelical and devotional, and much we enjoy it. The singing is touching to the Christian heart.

After service we sang several of our American hymns. After dinner I walk out alone, and enjoy the beauty of the scene and hold communion with God. It is a most lovely Sabbath to me; the clouds resting far down the mountain sides, and clinging round the summits, or floating high above all, are beautiful indeed.

In the evening we have service in the private

parlor of Mons. Deprezenski, and afterwards have an American service by ourselves, apart, and much enjoy the Sabbath in spiritual devotion. In the afternoon I walk up to a little summer house, and there hold fellowship with nature and God in his sublimest goings forth.

CHAPTER VI.

TRAVELS THROUGH ITALY AND GREECE—INTO TURKEY—SYRIA AND EGYPT—RETURNS HOME AND IS SENT BACK AS AGENT OF THE AMERICAN BIBLE SOCIETY.

It would be more than pleasant to me to follow him, or rather to go again with my friend through the remainder of this year's journey, revisiting the scenes that had such a charm for him, and are now to me invested with a sacred interest associated as they are with the memory of one who has "passed into the skies." Hand in hand we visited Genoa and Turin, and Milan, whose Cathedral Righter admired more than any building he saw in Europe; and he climbed to its roof before sunrise to see the first glory of the morning break on the distant mountain tops; and Venice where he was in a dream of delight in the silent streets and decaying palaces of that mysterious city; and Florence, in whose galleries of art we studied day after day, and at night enjoyed the society of friends from our own land; and Rome, once called the *Eternal* city, now the city of the Past; and Naples and its environs—the sepulchres of cities. And here we took ship again and touched at Malta, and then passed into Greece and climbed the Acropolis at Athens, and sojourned with Drs. King and Hill, and their families, and the Buels and the Arnolds, devoted Baptist missionaries there; and then we passed across the Archipelago and touched at Smyrna, and then went up the Hellespont into the Sea of Marmora, and visited the great city of the Orient, on the Golden Horn and the Bosphorus. What impressions this visit made upon him I would give in his own words, but his journals, during this tour, were never written up, and although voluminous, they are not complete. The sentences are imperfect and mere catchwords often used that were sufficiently suggestive to himself, but quite unintelligible to others. His visits among the families of the American missionaries in and around the city were delightful. He rejoiced in their work, and his heart was burning to be engaged in the same blessed labor.

One morning during our stay in Constantinople we were visiting the Bible House, where the Holy Scriptures, in fifteen or twenty different languages, are kept for sale. Righter and Hill were the companions of my walk this morning. While we were in the store, two Armenians, native preachers, came in and made a formal appeal to my two young friends, to remain in Constantinople and devote themselves to the Missionary cause. Or, if they could not now remain they were implored to take the subject into serious consideration, and if possible to revisit the East and spend their lives in this work. They received this appeal with much emotion. It was an unexpected and extraordinary call. It was not easy to respond to it at once, but they thought of it long and earnestly, and often recurred to it as one of the most interesting incidents in the East. It was not long after this, before Righter, obedient to clear manifestations of his duty, was on his way back again from his native country, to distribute the Word of God among the Armenians and Moslems, of the Levant. The coincidence is striking, that the call was first given to him in the BIBLE House, and in the specific work of BIBLE distribution he returned to Constantinople and laid down his life in Asia Minor.

We shall be with him here again and will not linger now. He passed on by steamer to Beyrut, and thence by land to Sidon, Tyre, Nazareth, and down to Jaffa. The unsettled state of the country rendering it unsafe to travel in the interior, we sailed from Jaffa to Alexandria, visited Cairo and the Pyramids, and then came home by way of Malta, Marseilles, Paris, London, and Liverpool.

Just one year had been spent in this journey. The great benefit to his eyes, and decided mental improvement he had received from the year of travel, gave zest and interest to the labors on which he was determined to enter. He would at once seek a pastoral settlement, and give himself wholly to the work.

The American Bible Society had for some time past been looking out for the man to take the place that had been so filled with so much efficiency and ability by the Rev. Simeon H. Calhoun, its agent in the Levant. Attention was drawn to the two young gentlemen who had just returned from the East, and had made themselves well acquainted with the field. There was work for both of them, and the subject was laid before them. Mr. Hill had already made up his mind to enter a field of labor at home, and he is now the faithful and able pastor of a church in Sheffield, Massachusetts.

Mr. Righter was urged to take the office and return at once to the Levant. There was but one objection that seemed to him insuperable—and that was his filial desire to remain and comfort his parents, now far advanced in life. He visited me in the country, and laid the whole case in my hands, begging me to tell him what was his duty in the premises, and declaring himself perfectly willing to go or stay, if he could be assured of the mind and will of his Father in heaven. That was more than I could show him; but I was strongly impressed with the conviction that his duty lay in the foreign field. His piety was above doubt. His energy with perseverance, and his zeal with prudence, were well tried and known. His heroic fortitude and his high enterprise would make him ready for bold and noble deeds of moral daring in the great work of giving the Bible to the Orient, and I confess I had strong desires that he should undertake the service.

He accepted the appointment, and was ordained by the Presbytery of Newark, in the city of Newark, N. J., to the work of the ministry.

CHAPTER VII.

MISSION TO THE EAST.

MR. RIGHTER left this country, for the last time as it proved, on the 30th of September, 1854. He sailed in the steamer Pacific, which was lost in the following year, having never been heard from after leaving port. A large number of his friends were on board to bid him farewell, in the confident hope of greeting him again after an absence of three years. He departed cheerfully, joyfully, to enter upon the great work that had been committed to him, that of disseminating the Word of God throughout that part of the world where it was first published, and where the gospel had its earliest triumphs. The voyage across the Atlantic was pleasant and prosperous. He writes to his mother, on board the

"STEAMER PACIFIC, Oct. 7th, 1854.

"MY DEAR MOTHER: How well I remember the last look of friends at parting, their farewell adieus on the wharf! How they linger with me still, by night and by day, as I sail upon the ocean, assuring me, in tenderness and love, that I do not go alone, but the Spirit and prayers of friends encompass me round in all my way. Though far on the wide waters I am not alone or lonely—the same stars gleam nightly in the sky as at home—the same moon shines out to cheer us on our voyage—the same God, who upholds the pillars of the land, doth likewise plant his footsteps in the mighty deep, and place around and underneath us his everlasting arms. He commands the winds and waves concerning us to bear us safely over the sea, and we thus go on our way rejoicing.

"I enjoy much the purity and poetry of the sea, the ideas of grandeur and sublimity it inspires, constantly mirroring to us God in his attributes of infinity and eternity, and lifting the soul away from earth to heaven. 'Whither shall we go from his presence, whither shall we fly from his Spirit? If we ascend into heaven he is there; if we make our bed in hell, behold, he is there; if we take the wings of the morning and dwell in the uttermost parts of the sea, even there shall his hand lead us, and his right hand uphold us.' Above, beneath, around, all speaks to us of him, the same ever-living, ever-acting, wonder-working God.

"We have had a delightful passage, speeding on through the ocean day after day, calm and tranquil as a May morning. Varying incidents are constantly occurring to interest and entertain. Now, we see a steamer in the distant horizon; now a vessel with all sails spread to the breeze, a splendid sight upon the wide ocean; and now a whale spouting the water high in air; and then an iceberg, an hundred and fifty feet above the water, resplendent as the sunlight falls upon it from afar. Then new and pleasant acquaintances are formed on board; new entertainments invented—games, concerts, and lectures—all to make the time flit quickly by, yet as the sun sinks in liquid, golden glory, behind the western wave, our thoughts ever turn toward home, and those we love in that far-off land. Indeed, the ties that bind us there seem to grow, at once, stronger and more tender as time and distance intervene the more between us."

Landing at Liverpool on the eleventh day, he proceeded the next morning to London. Here he called upon the officers of the British and Foreign Bible Society, who received him with great cordiality, promising to co-operate with the American Society in giving the Bible to the Eastern nations. He found that the British institution was printing an edition of five thousand copies for circulation at Constantinople and in the vicinity, and that it had a number already on deposit there, which could be brought into immediate use. The cordial reception which he met with from the friends of the Bible in London was very animating to his spirits, which were always buoyant and hopeful.

Here he spent one or two days in company with his friends, Rev. E. D. G. Prime, and Mr. D. E. Hawley, of New York, who had left home with him, and who were to be his travelling companions until they should reach Rome, where they were to separate. At Havre they were joined by Mr. Richard C. McCormick, Jr., Corresponding Secretary of the New York Young Men's Christian Association, who went with him to the Crimea, and subsequently left him at Constantinople. The time that they spent in the Isle of Wight was passed delightfully among the scenes of beauty and of interest with which that charming spot of earth abounds, the most interesting of which are the sacred places that have become familiar to the whole Christian world, through the sweet pages of Leigh Richmond's "Annals of the Poor," the cottage and the graves of the "Dairyman and his Daughter," and the home and burial-place of "Little Jane." In a letter to his brother he says:

"We made an excursion to the Isle of Wight, which we saw in the full perfection of autumnal beauty. Here we visited the grave and cottage of the 'Dairyman's Daughter;' saw the room in which she died, and the old Bible she used to read, with her name inscribed by her own hand; and then we went and stood beside the grave of 'Little Jane,' the young cottager, and felt our piety quickened and strengthened as we called to mind the life and death of these lambs of Christ's flock, who are now clothed with all the purity and holiness of heaven."

At Paris Mr. Righter, keeping the objects of his mission constantly in view, called upon several brethren interested in the Bible cause, from whom he learned many encouraging facts, not only relating to the circulation of the Scriptures in France, but especially in reference to the supply of the army going into the Crimea. The government had placed no obstacles in the way of furnishing the soldiers with the Bible, and the opportunity had been readily embraced as far as the funds in the hands of the Paris committee would allow. Dr. Grand Pierre, M. Presence, and Dr. Frederic Monod were especially interested in the objects he had in view.

At Geneva, in Switzerland, where he paused for two or three days, he called upon Dr. Cesar Malan, whom he had met on a previous visit; upon Dr. Merle D'Aubigné, and Col. Tronchin, who gave him much interesting information in reference to the efforts making for the spread of the Bible in Sardinia, in which the friends of the cause in Geneva were aided by funds from the American Bible Society. Here he also found the Rev. Mr. Whiting and his wife, missionaries to Syria, who had been spending the summer in Switzerland for the improvement of their health, and whom he had once met, and expected again to meet, on missionary ground. The Madiai family, who had well nigh proved martyrs to the reading of the Bible in Tuscany, were also sojourning in Geneva at the same time. Having been acquainted with them on his former visit to Europe, Mr. Righter renewed the acquaintance with heartfelt pleasure, sympathizing with them in the persecutions which they were called to endure, and as a representative of the friends of the Bible in this country, tendering to them the sympathy of Christians in America. This is, perhaps, the most appropriate place in which to insert a letter addressed to him by these exiled and suffering servants of Christ, in reply to one he had written from Constantinople about two months after this visit.

"Rue St. Antoine, Maison Boeri,
"Ancienne route de France, Feb. 2d, 1855.

"My Dear Sir: I feel most grateful to you for your kind remembrance of us, and very much obliged to your dear mother for the beautiful specimen of the silver-weed, as well as for the very appropriate verses which accompanied it. I shall preserve it carefully in my English Bible as a memento of Christian kindness and sympathy from the New World. It touches me much that Mrs. Righter should have given such an honorable place to such an unworthy gift.

"I regret to say that the Bible, *in question*, was taken with many other books by the Tuscan Government, and we have never been enabled to recover them; so that you see it is quite out of my power, unfortunately, to grant your request. I hope you will be so good as to mention this to Monsieur le Docteur Brigham.

"Two months back I took the liberty of writing to Mr. Cook, encouraged to do so by his having desired me, should I want anything, to address myself to him; as through the Lord's goodness I had not any personal favor to request, I ventured to ask his aid for an object which I have very much at heart, namely, the educating of four young girls (children of parents who have suffered for the truth), and who are to be afterwards employed, if the Lord will, as teachers in schools, in order to disseminate the pure light of the glorious gospel in this benighted land. I also asked his help to get some tracts printed in Italian, which have been already translated, and which we would have distributed in the mountains as well as in the towns of my native land. The funds we have are quite insufficient to complete either of these objects, they are more particularly under the direction of the Count Guicciardini, who is a well-known Christian, and extremely generous for everything which tends to promote the glory of his Lord and Master. A letter addressed here, to the Poste-Restante, to him, or to the Doctor Malan, at Geneva, would be sure to find them.

"My husband joins me in every kind wish for you and your mother, Mrs. Righter, and he desires me to salute you both in the words of the sixth chapter of Numbers, verses 24, 25, and 26.

"And again cordially thanking you for your welcome letter and acceptable present,

"I remain,

"Your humble servant in the Lord,

"FRANCESCO and

"ROSA MADIAI."

After pausing in Geneva Mr. Righter proceeded on his journey reaching Turin on the afternoon of Saturday, and left immediately for the Waldensian valley, where he spent the Sabbath, together with two friends, who were his travelling companions, Messrs. Prime and McCormick. This visit was one of deep interest to all who shared in its opportunities of Christian intercourse. The party arrived late in the evening at La Tour, but upon calling in the morning on the professors of the college they were warmly received, and the Sabbath, spent in communion and in worshipping with the Waldensian Christians, was one never to be forgotten. They were invited in the morning to walk out some two or three miles to one of the mountain churches, where they found the young men of the parish drawn up in martial array, fully equipped, as for an engagement. This had been their practice since the days when their fathers had to worship God in the constant apprehension that their persecutors might the next moment be upon them to silence the voice of prayer and of praise. It was a touching sight, on entering the little mountain chapel, to see the aged fathers and mothers assembled for the morning worship waiting in silence for it to commence, and with a devout and humble spirit entering heartily into the service. As one and another entered they stood for a few moments in silent prayer, and then sat down to unite in the service. Near this chapel, upon the mountain side, was a rock overhanging a precipice, from which, in the days of persecution, many victims of papal malice, chiefly women and little children, were thrown and cruelly murdered—a spot which awakens memories and emotions thrilling to every Protestant heart. But it was a pleasure to these Protestants from the New World to find the children of the persecuted, and the children of the Most High, enjoying such peace and prosperity, where their forefathers had suffered the most inhuman cruelties, and where myriads had suffered martyrdom, for no other crime than that of rejecting the idolatries of the Romish Church.

In the afternoon these friends attended the parish church at La Tour, and in the evening met the professors and students of the college, and enjoyed some hours of most delightful Christian intercourse, which was closed by addresses expressive of the mutual interest which this interview had afforded.

After spending the following day in pleasant intercourse with Dr. Revel, then Moderator of the Waldensian Synod, and with other Christian friends, the party returned to Turin. Here Mr. Righter was visited at his hotel by a number of Italians, who, having learned that his visit was in behalf of the Bible, earnestly importuned assistance in circulating it throughout Sardinia and other portions of Italy. Thus, at every step in his journey, he met with encouragement in regard to the great work upon which he had set out. The same, to a limited extent, was true even in Florence, where the imprisonment of the Madiai had suppressed all public efforts to circulate the Word of God. Even at Rome he was not without encouraging evidence that the Word of God was circulated to some extent, and that it was desired by many more.

Touching at Malta, on his way East, he had conferences with the English residents in regard to the work and its progress. Hearing that the cholera was raging at Athens, and that he could not accomplish anything material toward carrying out the object of his mission until the next season, he determined to sail directly to Constantinople. On the voyage, November 26, he makes the following note in his journal:

"It is a lovely morning. We have an hour of communion, and social worship together in our state-room, McCormick, Wortabed, and myself. The Assyrian seems to have a tender and warm Christian heart. We had a pleasant converse together. Read Psalms xci., xcvi.; John xiv.; Rev. i."

Mr. Righter spent a day at Smyrna, where he saw several of the missionary and other brethren, and reached Constantinople December 1st. It appeared as if the time of his coming was not the most auspicious, owing to the existence of the war, and the disturbed state of the Eastern world in consequence. But he soon found that a spirit of inquiry was beginning to prevail extensively among the people of the country, and that the presence of four large armies of itself opened a vast and interesting field for the circulation of the Bible. Mr. Barker, the agent of the British and Foreign Bible Society, had already commenced the supply of the soldiers and sailors connected with the British army and shipping, and those in the hospitals, both sick and wounded. Mr. Righter at once entered with him into this work, visiting the hospitals, and having access to those on their way to the Crimea.

On the 6th of December a meeting of the Constantinople Bible Society was held. The American minister, Mr. Spence, presided, and made the opening address, urging the circulation of the Bible as the most effectual means of promoting peace and good will among men. Rev. Mr. Thompson, the Secretary, read the report, from which it appeared that much had been accomplished in the supply of the English and French armies, and even of the Russian prisoners of war. Addresses were also made by American and English clergymen present, and officers of the English army and navy, and by Mr. Righter, as a representative of the American Bible Society, who assured them of the cordial co-operation of that Society in giving the Bible to all the dwellers and sojourners in the East. The meeting was held in the hall of the principal hotel, and was attended by a large assembly of ladies and gentlemen, who listened for three hours with unabated interest to the proceedings and addresses. The effect of the meeting was to give still greater encouragement to all engaged or interested in the cause.

On the 12th of December a meeting of the Committee of the Auxiliary Bible Society was held. Mr. Kumberlach presided, and made some very interesting statements in reference to the Russian prisoners. They received the Testaments gladly, and one officer in particular, who had killed a number of English, earnestly besought the gift of a Testament, and others joined in the same request. This led to a motion recommending the publication of the Old Testament in modern Russe.

Mr. Righter describes one of his visits to the English hospital, where the wounded, some having lost arms and others legs, and others wasted with long sickness and suffering, were lying in great numbers, but all at length well provided for. He says, "The Testament is placed within the reach of all, and I saw many of them attentively reading it as I passed. I called upon the chief surgeon, who gives his sanction and encouragement to the circulation of the Bible, and then upon Miss Nightingale. Was delighted with her benevolent expression and gentle spirit. She received me very kindly, and thanked me for the interest that is felt in America in her benevolent enterprise, and in the suffering English soldiers. She has distributed many Testaments. The Roman Catholics receive them gladly, but the priests interfered. She requests the Douay version for them. They have 3,000 sick and wounded here, and are expecting 1,000 more from the camp."

CHAPTER VIII.

VISIT TO THE CRIMEA.

HAVING accomplished all that required immediate attention in connexion with the Bible cause at Constantinople, Mr. Righter determined upon making a visit to the camp of the allied armies at Sebastopol, to ascertain by personal inspection what opening there might be for the circulation of the Holy Scriptures among the troops. Accordingly he called upon Admiral Boxer to obtain an order or permit to visit the Crimea, which was cheerfully given as soon as the object of the visit was made known. Mr. Righter hastily packed up about a hundred Bibles and Testaments for his own personal distribution, and in company with his friend, Mr. McCormick, on the 21st of December, went on board the transport steamer Medway, bound for the Crimea.

An account of his visit is given in his own words, taken from a letter to the editors of the "New York Observer." It is a graphic description of the horrors of war, and of the desolation which it leaves in its track.

"CAMP BEFORE SEBASTOPOL, December 24, 1854.

"MESSRS. EDITORS: It was thought desirable that I should visit the Crimea for the purpose of making arrangements to supply the English and French troops with the Bible. We are in camp before Sebastopol, on the field of Inkerman, within the roar of the enemy's cannon, and in the midst of shot and shell flying and bursting on either side. The officer who entertains me was engaged in the battle, and he walks with me a few steps upon the hill and points out the field. 'This,' said he, 'where we are now standing is the famous sand-bag battery which was taken and re-taken three times in the engagement, and here the Russians and English lay in heaps together. There the Cossacks came up the valley at half-past six in the morning 60,000 strong to surprise our little band of only 8,000 men, and we fought them, hand to hand, with sword, pistol, and bayonet, for four hours, when we began to feel that we must soon be overpowered by numbers and entirely cut off to a man; but the timely relief of the French, under General Bosquet, revived our drooping courage—we charged down the hill—soon put them to flight and drove them from the field, and the French closely pursued them even within the walls of Sebastopol. But what a terrible sight it was the afternoon and evening after the battle, to see the dead and dying strewn over the field, mangled and cut to pieces! and then to hear the moan of the wounded and suffering as it sounded in our ears. Our tents, too, were all riddled and torn by balls and shot from their cannon and musketry, and our poor fellows were groaning for assistance. And we scarcely dare walk among the wounded, for the savage Russians, just able to crawl, would bayonet and shoot our men, as they were giving a cup of cold water to their suffering comrades. They even fired upon us from their batteries when we were burying their own dead upon the field. The next day we buried a thousand Russians in one grave, and when we came to one Englishman, our men said, "He must not go in with the Cossacks." I said, "Yes, they will now surely sleep quietly side by side," and we put him in too, and one grave closed over them all. I never saw a battle before, and never wish to see another. It was awful beyond conception.'

"Such is the description given me by one who was eye-witness and took part in this terrible conflict. I then proposed to walk across a little ravine to an adjoining height, where I could have a good view of Sebastopol.

"'Yes,' said he, 'I think it can be done now with safety, there is less firing than usual this afternoon, I would go with you, but I am on double duty and cannot leave the camp. Be careful and not get beyond our entrenchments. Lord

Dunkellin was taken prisoner by a party of Russians just below this.'

"After a refreshing cup of tea, I retired for the night. There had been cheering along the lines in the evening, and we thought it might be a signal for the assault which was daily expected, and as you might well imagine, my dreams were filled with sounds of cheers, and charge, and all the excitement of battle. Nor was it all a dream, for the Russians made a sortie upon the trenches, and there was a heavier cannonading than usual that night, which shook the ground and tent around me. In the morning I was aroused early by the notes of the bugle, and beating of the morning drum to order and to arms for their daily drill. The music sounds beautifully through the encampment. The whole camp is soon astir, and formed in line, and as we ride along four miles in front, it presents a brilliant scene, with all the pomp and circumstance of war. We have now reached the extreme left of the English defence, and another officer wishes to accompany us for the purpose of giving us 'the best possible view of Sebastopol and the entrenchments.' We walk a few steps to a height above the camp, and thence, with a good glass, can look directly into the town, the fortifications and batteries in front of the walls, and it indeed seems as if the Allies had not made the least impression upon it. As our friends themselves assured us, 'it is stronger now than when they first began the siege, for the Russians have speedily repaired every damage, and have even erected mud batteries outside the walls to fire upon our lines.'

"'Now,' said they, 'if you will walk half a mile farther in front we will give you a still nearer view.' So we descended into a deep ravine called 'The Valley of Death,' and here the shot and shell, thirteen inch, and twenty-four and fifty-six pounders, lay like hailstones covering the ground, most of which, we were told, had been thrown from the Russian batteries during the first day of the bombardment, but now occasionally one is added to the number, not a very comfortable announcement. We then ascended the height, and here we could not only see the streets and buildings of the town, and the whole line of fortifications and entrenchments, but also the flash of the evening guns, and could hear the shells whizzing through the air and bursting around us. The English were firing from their battery a few rods below, and the French had just opened a new battery a short distance to the left; and the Russians were answering their fire from the town. I asked, 'Is it not rather dangerous here?' 'Yes,' said they, 'a chance shot might strike us, or it would not be surprising if the Russians should direct a shell toward us, seeing a little company together with spy-glasses in our hands.' We then rode across a large ravine, and came to the French camp. They occupy the extreme left or south side of the town, while the English hold the position to the right and north. The French have advanced much nearer the walls with their trenches than the English, and say they will be the first to make the assault and enter the town, and that they will even go in alone if the English are not ready to join them. From this point we had a fine view of the allied fleet lying off Cape Chersonese, watching the movements of the Russians, though they do not venture to enter the harbor and risk a hand-to-hand engagement with them.

"So I set out alone to cross the valley and ascend the hill; and then I saw another hill beyond, where a still better view might be obtained, and having gained this, I could see the Russian fleet, Fort Constantine, the narrow entrance of the harbor, where they have sunk their ships, the walls and fortifications of the town, with perfect distinctness. Yet I saw another height beyond, still nearer, and was advancing toward it when I suddenly came upon a dead Russian lying beside his horse upon the field, and then another near by, and cannon balls and shells were now scattered thick around, and the dogs, preying upon the dead horses, began to bark at me, and the battery opened its fire, sending large shells whizzing through the air. Just then, too, I looked down into the ravine below, and saw a suspicious-looking party of men, and all at once it flashed upon me that I had probably gone beyond the English lines. I immediately beat a retreat and hastened back to the camp, where I related the adventure to my friend. It was wise that I had returned, for, said he, the enemy's advance battery is just there, and the Cossacks frequently come over the hill, in reconnoitring parties.

"It is now evening and quite too late to return to-night to Balaklava, seven miles distant. I therefore accepted my friend's kind invitation to spend the night in his tent. We have very plain fare, cold salt pork, hard sea-biscuit, and coffee that is picked green and roasted, and pounded fine with large stones, and this at the table of a commissioned officer in the English army, yet I relished it well since it was most heartily given. As it is clear moonlight I spend an hour in visiting the soldiers in their tents. I found one or more sick and suffering in almost every tent, wrapped in blankets, and lying on the cold, damp ground. They complained of want of warm winter-clothing and suitable provisions, having nothing but salt meat and no wood to cook it, stale pilot-biscuit, and green coffee, and no fire to roast it, and no medical attendance whatever, and yet they are obliged to lie out in the trenches at night exposed to the wet and cold, and in constant fear of attack from the enemy. The night before six had been frozen to death there, and the night before that the Russians had made a sortie upon them and bayoneted ten others. 'Our sufferings are very great,' said they, 'but we are ready to meet the Cossacks at any moment, and die for the glory of our country.' I could not but have a great sympathy for the poor, brave fellows. I spoke a kind word of encouragement, and distributed a few Bibles and Testaments to them, which they received with much gratitude and thankfulness of heart.

"As I returned home to my tent, the view of the encampment, stretching for miles along the hillsides and in the valleys around, and the watch-fires blazing upon the heights afar, were picturesque and beautiful. My worthy host meets me at the door of his tent, 'Do you see,' said he, 'that smoke curling in the distance? You see, then, how near we are to our enemies. That is the smoke of the Russian camp. They have a battery just across the ravine, and they frequently open their fire upon us, though they have been silent for some time past. Their men and ours often go down to this stream and water their horses on opposite sides.'

"I then proceeded to head-quarters, and called

upon Lord Raglan in behalf of the American Bible Society. He received me very kindly, and invited me to dine with him on the following day. At his table I had the pleasure of meeting the officers of his staff, and an English lady, the Hon. Miss Derryman, who had come to the Crimea to visit her brother, a young officer wounded at Inkerman. His lordship asked me many questions about America, and was much interested, as they all were, to know the feelings of Americans in reference to the war.

"His Lordship lives in a large house appropriated to the purpose, about two miles from the front camp, and maintains grand style with his suite of apartments, and silver plate and service. The houses and stables for his grooms and horses, the large marquées of his officers, and the guard-tents pitched around with flags floating from them, form quite a military settlement and a gay scene.

"But it was now getting late, and his Lordship inquired, 'If we certainly knew the road to Balaklava, five miles distant,' saying, 'the path was quite uncertain at night.' We replied with some degree of assurance, took leave of his lordship, and set out on our way. But we had not proceeded far before a thick fog arose, and soon darkness closed around us. My friend, who assumed to be the guide of our party, said it was now all confused to him. He knew not whether we were going right towards, or right from, our point of destination, and we were beyond the line of tents, and saw camp-fires far in the distance. As we rode on, however, we saw an object just before us that appeared like a sentinel at his post. We knew not whether he was Cossack or friend, yet we ventured to hail him with the watchwords, 'Who goes there?' ('Qui vive') and no answer was returned; but as we advanced still nearer, we found he was a *stray horse*, and could, therefore, give us no direction in the road. We rode on another half hour, and then saw a company of men on the hill above us, yet were in doubt whether they were friends or Cossacks; we slowly drew near and listened to their voices, and could not distinguish whether they were speaking Turkish or Russian. But we had lost our way, and must summon up courage to hail them. Happily they proved to be French, on their road to the camp, and, with the politeness of Frenchmen, directed us in the right path. We had not proceeded a half hour, however, before we found ourselves again in the brushwood, quite out of the path; but fortunately, we once more heard voices in the ravine below, and this was a little company of Irish soldiers, who had also lost their way, and were pitching their tent for the night. Said I, 'Can you direct me the way to Balaklava?' One of them at once accompanied me up the hill, and said, 'This is the road, sir.' 'Are you quite sure?' I asked. 'An' faith, I am certain, sir, for I have just come it myself.' Thus encouraged, we rode on with lightsome hearts; presently the moon shone out in clear sky to cheer us on our way, and then we saw the Highland camp in the valley below to guide us forward, and in one hour more we reached Balaklava and our good ship in safety, with much rejoicing and gratitude of heart.

"It is impossible to describe the state of the roads and country trodden and trampled down in every direction. The work of war. The landmarks are removed, the trees cut down, the houses torn down, and the furniture, even chairs, pianos, and sofas, everything consumable has been used for fuel by the army. It was indeed a beautiful country when the Allies first landed, abounding in vineyards, cultivated fields, and lovely country residences; now it is a waste of perfect desolation. The heavy rains and dragging of artillery, have made the mud half knee deep, and the horses, by being overworked, are dying by hundreds in the fields, and even the men are sinking down by the roadside, and dying under their heavy burdens, for as the horses have failed, they are obliged to transport their provisions, and even their heavy fifty-six pound shot and shell, to the camp on the backs of men. There is great suffering too in the front camp, for want of stores and warm clothing. They are dying there at the rate of sixty per day, and coming down sick to the Hospital at Balaklava more than a hundred a day. And with the Turks it is still worse. It even amounts to a plague among them. They are dying by fifties, emaciated and loathsome in the extreme; you see them lying dead and borne on litters in every direction for burial; cast in pits, and loose dirt or stones thrown upon them. It is dreadful to behold.

"The French, on the contrary, are better furnished with clothing, provisions, and medical attendance; they have fresh bread every other day in their camp, warm tents and fires, yet such is the severity of the season here, and so great is the exposure in the trenches at night and from rain and snow, that the mortality among *them* is also very great.

"Thus the Czar has likewise two powerful allies, winter and disease, which are making fearful ravages among the allied troops. Reinforcements are rapidly arriving from France and England, but the new troops are dying faster than the old ones, who have been longer here, and are hardened to the exposure. The Allies occupy fifteen miles of defence, constantly exposed to attack from the Russians, who are near their lines on all sides, and have free communication with the fleet and fortress of Sebastopol, as well as their provinces by the way of Perekop on the north. The Allies have 100,000 men and 650 heavy guns, while the Russian army has 150,000 men, and 700 guns of larger size than the Allies, as well as the advantage of strong fortifications, and ammunition for two years. I also notice that the Czar has just issued a ukase for a new levy of one man to every thousand in his empire, which will increase his army more than a million. So that there must be terrible fighting yet, and there is every prospect that Sebastopol will not be taken at least before next Spring.

"The most perfect good feeling exists between the French and English on the part of soldiers and officers; they salute each other with the common term, 'buono Inglese,' 'buono Francese,' good English, good French, and both equally detest and despise the Turks, kicking and beating them like Turkish dogs, as they themselves formerly treated the Christians. I myself saw a Turkish officer, with his face all cut and bleeding from the sword of an English soldier, who escaped with a slight reprimand, whereas if the offence had been committed against an English or French officer, by a Turkish soldier, he would have been immediately shot.

"I would also add that my esteemed friend, Mr. Richard C. McCormick, Jr., Secretary of the Young Men's Christian Association of New York, who has been my travelling companion from Paris to the East, likewise acompanied me to the Crimea, and has been of essential service to me in my efforts in behalf of the soldiers. His health still continues good.

"Most sincerely your friend,

"C. N. RIGHTER."

CHAPTER IX.

BIBLE LABORS IN THE CRIMEA.

THE letter given below was addressed to the Secretary of the American Bible Society, and contains a deeply interesting record of the perseverance and the success of Mr. Righter in his efforts to secure the distribution of the Bible in the allied armies of England and France.

"CAMP BEFORE SEBASTOPOL, Dec. 26, 1854.

"MY DEAR BROTHER: As I found that all the avenues for Bible distribution among the soldiers and sailors at Constantinople were occupied by the agency of the British and Foreign Bible Society, I decided with the advice and approbation of our good friends, to make a visit to the camp at Sebastopol, for the purpose of ascertaining the demand there, and making arrangements for the supply. Accordingly I was kindly presented with an order from Admiral Boxer for a passage on board an English transport ship to the Crimea. It was a lovely afternoon as we sailed from the Golden Horn through the Bosphorus out to the Black Sea, and thence two days upon its stormy waters to Balaklava, the fine little harbor for English shipping and stores for the army of the East. I took a hundred Bibles and Testaments with me, and on my arrival was received by Mr. Matheson, agent of the Soldier's Friend Society, who gave me a cordial welcome, and remarked that my visit there at the present time was most providential, and I could have brought nothing more acceptable than Bibles. He said, however, there was great opposition on the part of the chief chaplain to any religious effort in behalf of the soldiers. He himself had been forbidden the camp by this authority, and whatever he was able to accomplish must be done in the most clandestine manner possible. And as I accompanied him in his benevolent work, I soon found it was but too true. He seemed afraid to let it be known that he had tracts or religious books. He kept them concealed under his coat and in his pockets, and as he met the soldiers singly or in little companies off duty, he would secretly slip a tract or religious book into their hands for them to carry to their tents and read. Yet I was glad to notice how thankfully all received them at his hands. 'Don't you see,' said he, 'how guarded I must be not to attract attention from the officers or chaplains in my work, or I would be immediately expelled from the field; yet I am daily distributing my hundreds of tracts, and they are doing their good work in the army and navy.' I asked if it were not possible for me to obtain permission from the officers for the distribution of the Bible among the troops. 'There is not the least possibility of it,' said he. 'I would not advise you to call upon them for that purpose, it will only excite their opposition.'

"I then called upon Rev. Mr. Hayward, the chaplain of the royal forces at Balaklava. He received me very kindly, and said that Bibles were much needed by the soldiers, but to how great an extent he knew not. He had received a small supply from England, and had only given them sparingly, and thought many more might be wanted. I found him to be a man of excellent Christian spirit, denying himself the ordinary comforts and enjoyments of life, and laboring night and day for the spiritual welfare of the suffering and dying soldiers. And it was delightful to see how kindly these rough soldiers received his visits, and listened to the words of love and Christian admonition he addressed them. He seemed fully imbued with the spirit of our Savior, 'who went about doing good.' Yet when I proposed, in accompanying him on his visit, to give a few Bibles and Testaments to those who desired them, he replied at once, 'It is contrary to general orders, and I would not dare give my consent.'

I then asked if it were not possible to obtain such authority from the commander-in-chief. He said, 'You may make the effort, but I am quite sure you will not succeed. I should be right glad if it were so.' Notwithstanding, I set out next morning early for headquarters at the camp, four miles distant, putting a few Testaments in my pocket for distribution by the way. As we were trudging along through the mud half-knee deep (it is impossible to conceive the state of the roads which the heavy rains and artillery wagons have made), I saw the wife of a soldier, in the midst of the din and confusion of the scene, stopping to rest by the wayside, and her interesting countenance attracted my attention. I stepped forward, spoke a pleasant word to her, and asked her if she had a Bible or Testament in her tent. 'Oh, no,' said she, 'we have just come from Varna, and if you could give me one I should be very thankful;' and an old soldier coming up, said, 'If you could give me one, too, sir, I would think very much of it. I belong to Captain Frazer's battery, and we have no Bibles there.' So I gave them each one, and went on my way rejoicing. In two hours we reached the headquarters of Lord Raglan. Here I called upon General Estcourt, his principal secretary, and stated the object of my visit, in the name of the American Bible Society, to obtain permission to supply the soldiers of the army with

Bibles and Testaments. He received me very kindly, and said he would at once present the subject to Lord Raglan, who would undoubtedly grant my request.

"I then proceded to 'headquarters' of the French General, Canrobert, for a like purpose in reference to the French troops, stating that the Emperor had given such permission for the camp at Boulogne, and in France Bibles were stamped for general circulation by authority of government. His aide-de-camp kindly offered to take the matter in charge, and send me the General's answer next morning. Subsequently I called upon Lord Raglan in person. He gave me a very gracious reception, and invited me to dine with him on the morrow, when he would have a written communication prepared. Accordingly, the next day I had the pleasure of dining with his Lordship and staff, and of receiving from his secretary the following letter:

"'CAMP BEFORE SEBASTOPOL, Dec. 28, 1854.

"'SIR: I have this afternoon seen Lord Raglan, and have communicated to him the desire of the American Bible Society, and the purpose of your visit to Balaklava at this time. I am directed by his Lordship to express the thanks which are due from the army to the American Bible Society for their benevolent intentions, and to say that his

Lordship can have no objection to the distribution of Bibles to the soldiers of this army; quite the contrary; but he thinks it desirable that it should be intrusted to the chaplains of the army attached to the different divisions, or at any rate, that it may be done in concert with them, so that they may be made acquainted with all that is done.

"'If it should happen that the Society should wish to send a gentleman of their body to watch the distribution of their bounty, I must request that he will first call on me, bringing with him the authority of the Society for acting in their behalf.

"'I have the honor to be, sir,

"'Your most obedient servant,

"'J. BUCKNALL ESTCOURT, A. J.

"'The Rev. C. N. Righter.'

"The Society understand, I hope, that the distribution of Bibles cannot be allowed to entail any sort of ministration to the soldiers. I have to add, that I received yesterday evening a note from Major Clairmont, attached to the headquarters of the French army, and he begs me to say that your views in respect to the French army would be contrary to their rules, and therefore that the General Canrobert must decline to give his sanction to your request.

"His Lordship likewise remarked he was very

happy such a benevolent work was designed on the part of the American Bible Society, and hoped it would still further have an influence to promote good feeling and Christian fellowship between England and America. Whereupon I took my leave, thanking his Lordship cordially for his kind expressions and entertainment. I then proceeded at once with the letter in hand (having 'War,' and 'on Her Majesty's Service,' printed upon it in large capitals) to the advance camp in front of Sebastopol, there to ascertain whether the soldiers really needed Bibles, and how they would receive them. It was evening when I arrived. The cannonading from the town was unusually heavy that night, and shot and shell were firing and bursting on either side of us, though providentially none reached our camp. In the course of our conversation, the officer who entertained me remarked, he had lost his Bible that he brought with him from England, and a good lady at Constantinople had given him another, which he valued very much. I then said, that was the object of my visit, to learn if there were not other officers and soldiers who also wished the Bible. He did not doubt I would find many such. Thus encouraged I set out by moonlight to walk around our little cluster of tents, comprising one division only, while the whole encampment stretches fifteen miles along the hillsides, and through the ravines around. In the first tent I entered there were three soldiers, and when I inquired if they were all supplied with Bibles and Testaments, one poor fellow, lying on the damp ground wrapped in his blanket, raising himself up, said, 'I would like very much to have one, sir;' then the others expressed the same desire; and as I gave them each a Testament they thanked me with heartfelt gratitude for coming so far to give them the Word of Life; and would not let me go without receiving some gifts of nuts and almonds from them in return. In the next tent I found three others, and one of them shivering with the ague; and upon repeating the same question, he roused up, and said, 'I would like very much to have a Bible: I had one when I left England, but I lost it at the battle of Alma; and since then I have had nothing but a prayer-book, which I plundered from the knapsack of a dead comrade at Inkerman.' I accordingly offered him a Bible, remarking that it was our custom to sell to those who were able to buy, and give freely to those who were not. 'I have money,' said he, 'and would gladly pay for it: I should value it the more. How much shall I give?' I said, 'Whatever you choose.' He handed me at once 3*s.* 6*d.* sterling, or seven shillings in our money. I gave him back twenty-five cents, saying it was too much for a poor soldier to pay. 'Oh, no,' said he, 'keep it all. *I give it all as a free-will offering to the American Bible Society.*' I gave the others Testaments, and as I left they pronounced many blessings on my head, for bringing them the Word of God, saying, 'the last thing they would throw away again on their march would be the *Bible.*' In the next tent I met with a like reception. One soldier said he wished to have a Bible, 'and,' said he, 'I rather think I will take two; for I am quite sure my brother, who is out on duty in the trenches, would like to have one also;' and he handed me out 4*s.*, or one dollar of our money, saying he was very thankful to receive them for that; and one, sitting beside him, politely took off his cap to me, and said, 'Now I can enjoy the Word of God too; for though I cannot read myself, I can hear it from this man, and it will do me as much good as him. We have been in all the battles together, and, thank God, we have both been preserved. But can you not come to-morrow night, when the others will be in from the pickets? I am sure they would all like to get Bibles of you. Oh, sir, if we could only have the like of you to come and see us in our tents, and speak a kind word to us, how thankful we would be!' I was pleased, too, to notice the respectfulness as well as kindness with which they received me, a stranger, bearing the Bible. I remarked, 'The medals voted by Parliament for those engaged at Alma and Inkerman are coming soon.' 'Yes,' said they, 'and we will be glad to get them; but we would rather have *your Bibles.*' I said, 'Then I hope you will read and treasure them, as the Word of God which maketh us wise unto everlasting salvation.' 'Never fear that,' says one, 'I have a sister at home, who sends me a good tract every time she writes to me; and I have read and kept them every one, and now I have the Bible, which is better than all.' As my little stock was thus so soon exhausted, I returned to my tent, rejoiced that I had been privileged to distribute Bibles and Testaments to those noble soldiers in camp on the field of Inkerman, and prayed that God would abundantly bless his Word to their spiritual good.

"In the morning early, at the beating of the morning drum, I hastened down to Balaklava, where my good friends were delighted to hear of my unexpected success, both with officers and soldiers, and they heartily thanked God for it. Rev. Mr. Hayward said at once he would take 1,000 Bibles and Testaments for distribution, and would send us in return a part of his stated collection at the church service. Rev. Mr. Campbell also wished 600, and many more would be required by the other chaplains. Mr. Matheson also begged that he might be constituted agent for the work, as he regarded it even more important than distributing tracts, to circulate the Book of God. 'And,' said he to me, 'we have the Word; now we only want the Spirit; we must have earnest prayer for that.'

"I then called upon the chief of police, for the purpose of obtaining access to the Russian prisoners, and supplying them with the Bible. I found the officer himself was out, but his deputy was sitting behind the desk, and it seems he had received intimation that I was coming, for he asked immediately, 'What is it you wish, sir? Is it anything I can do as well? I rather think it is something in the missionary line, isn't it?' I replied, 'Yes; I wished to see the Russian prisoners, and give them the Bible, if they desired it.' 'Well,' said he, 'I always like to help on the good Cause, and will be glad to accompany you.'

"We accordingly took with us an interpreter, and proceeded to the guard-house. The sentinels on duty demanded our business. He stepped forward and said, 'We wish to see the Russian prisoners. This man is a missionary: this is Mr. Upton, and I am deputy-provost; and whatever is done well, or whatever is done ill, I will be answerable for it.' The sentinels immediately stood aside, and we entered the guard-room. Here were eleven prisoners, only one of whom could read; and upon asking him if he would like to receive a new Testament, he expressed great desire to have it, and when I gave it in his hand he manifested much thankfulness, and said, he would not only read it himself, but would also read it aloud to the others that the Word of God might be multiplied. The officer insisted upon it that he must receive and value it as the Book of Salvation, and he replied with many expressions of gratitude for so precious a gift. And when I thanked the officer for his kind assistance in the matter, 'Not at all,' said he, 'these things do me as much good as you.' And I am happy to add that I have received the same generous aid, in furtherance of my Bible efforts, from all the English officers in every department of the service. I then obtained an order from the commissariat for a return passage, and in two days reached Constantinople, where I gave a full report of my visit before the committee of the Auxiliary Bible Society, which held its meeting on Tuesday last, and so great was the interest manifested, that it was at once voted that we jointly send a colporteur to labor in that important field. I have also written to Paris, to gain permission from the Emperor for a like work of Bible distribution among the French troops, which I doubt not will be readily granted."

"CONSTANTINOPLE, Jan. 4, 1855.

"This morning I have sent a small supply of Bibles and Testaments to the chaplains at the Crimea for immediate distribution, instructing that they be sold, in each instance, where the soldiers are willing to purchase, and only given in special cases of need. I find Mr. Barker, agent of the British and Foreign Bible Society here, a most excellent and efficient man; with whom I can entirely harmonize and co-operate in all my Bible movements.

"Yesterday I received a letter from Dr. King, at Athens, giving an account of the terrible ravages of cholera there for the last two months, and fully approving the wisdom of my decision in coming directly to Constantinople, as besides the great exposure of life, I could have accomplished absolutely nothing there. He adds, moreover, that the work of issuing the modern Greek New Testament has been delayed at least two months by reason of the scourge. I deeply regret to announce the sudden death of Mrs. Everett of this mission, since I last wrote, cordially beloved by all who knew her—taken from us in the midst of youth and active usefulness, and leaving a bereaved husband and tender, sorrowing family to mourn her loss. Such are the inscrutable ways of Providence to man. Yet we bow submissively to his afflictive hand, and feel to say, 'He doeth all things well;' 'The Lord gave, and the Lord hath taken away, blessed be the name of the Lord.'

"Most sincerely yours,
"in the bonds of the Bible,
"C. N. RIGHTER."

CHAPTER X.

BIBLE LABORS IN TURKEY.

MR. RIGHTER reached Constantinople, on his return from the Crimea, on the last day of the year 1854. Besides attending to the distribution of the Scriptures in the hospitals and among the various classes in the city and vicinity, he commenced an effort to obtain a depository for Bibles and other religious books, which was soon successful. In a letter to the American Bible Society, dated April 19th, 1855, he speaks of the opening and of the encouragements to the circulation of the Scriptures as follows:

"The principal feature of interest in connexion with the Bible cause at Constantinople, during the present month, is the opening of our new depository to the public, for the sale of Bibles in various languages, in Pera, the Frank quarter of the city. We have obtained a large magazine in the main street, and erected a sign over the door with 'Bible and Religious Book Depository' in large capitals upon it, and suspended another in front with five different languages, English, French, German, Turkish, and Greek, upon the two sides; and placed the open Bible in various tongues in the windows, announcing to the multitude of every nation, who throng this crowded street, that 'here each in his own language can buy the Bible.' And it is most interesting to notice them stopping to read a moment in passing, and then coming in to buy the Word of God. A few days since four Bulgarians came and purchased the Psalms in Russian; then came a Jew and bought a Spanish Bible, and another the Old Testament in Hebrew; then an Italian called for the Bible, and a Greek, and Armenian, and German, and several French officers also wished for Bibles; and all freely gave their money in exchange for the Book of Life. We have likewise included other religious books, and connected a small reading-room with the establishment, in order to bring more in contact with the Scriptures, and thereby increase their sale; and this has operated thus far most successfully.

"The whole is under the direction of a committee, of which Count de Zuylon Van Neyvelt, the Ambassador of Holland, is president, a man of most earnest and excellent Christian spirit.

"We have received a letter from the British and Foreign Bible Society, expressing their willingness to pay a reasonable proportion of the expenses of the depository for the sale of their books, and the committee have voted that they be requested to grant the sum of £50, as their proportion of the expense of the institution for the present year. I have already written to the American Bible Society upon the subject. Thus a new and most important agency is established for the spread of the Bible in this great metropolis, and incidentally to the various cities and towns of the Ottoman empire."

In the same letter he makes mention of the remarkable spirit of inquiry after the Word which had sprung up among the Turks:

"In my last two letters I have spoken of the remarkable interest the Turks are beginning to manifest in the Bible. This is increasing. Three Turks recently came to the depository at Stamboul, and bought each a Bible, saying that 'they regarded it as a treasure above price;' and two others, upon receiving the Bible, kissed it devoutly, and pressed it to their bosom, to express their love for it as the only true revelation from God, and opening to them the only true way of salvation. And another, as he bought the Bible, remarked that, 'it was a very excellent book, but it came from the Turks.' They still persist in believing that nothing good can come from the

Christians. Said he, 'Many hundred years ago, when we conquered the city, we found this book here in one of the magazines, and we did not value it very much. A short time afterwards an English traveller came along, and we sold it to him for a trifle. He took it home, and translated it into English. And this is the same Bible in Turkish, which you Christians have brought to us. It is our book, and we prize it highly.'

"Also another Turk has, of his own accord, proposed to open a shop for the sale of Turkish Bibles and Testaments in the midst of the other bazaars of the city, which would attract the attention of all. This is surely very wonderful, when we remember that, according to the Mohammedan law, for a Mussulman to receive the Bible and become a Christian, is still punishable with death, which penalty has been executed within the last year at Adrianople, only three days' distant from the capital.

"A few days since I called upon Lord Stratford de Redcliffe, English Ambassador at the Sublime Porte, who has always been the firm friend of the Bible Cause and Protestantism in the East, and expressed to him the acknowledgments of our Society for the aid his protection and influence have always afforded us in publishing and distributing the Bible in the Ottoman empire. He received me very kindly, and replied: 'Our cause and interest are the same. We are always glad to protect Americans and American missionaries where our consular authority extends, and yours does not. The American missionaries are most excellent men.' Said he, 'To what church do you belong?' I said that 'I was a Presbyterian, but that our Society embraced all evangelical denominations.' 'I wish,' said he, 'that we could all adopt the Apostles' 'creed,' and have no further divisions into churches and sects.' I replied, 'That was precisely the creed and spirit of the American Bible Society.'"

Under a later date he writes:

"The Turks still continue to manifest a remarkable interest in the Bible and New Testament, and are calling for these at our magazines. As I was sitting in the depository a few days since, my attention was attracted to an old Turk with a long beard, who was reading very intently in the open Bible through the window. He afterward came in and asked to have one showed to him, saying, 'Eyi, chok eyi' (Good, very good).

"Also a Softa, one of the readers of the Koran at the mosques, came and begged that a Bible might be given him, which was accordingly done, with the prayer that his eyes might thereby be opened, and he be led to renounce the corrupt system of the false prophet, and embrace the truth as it is in Jesus."

The same inquiry came from various parts of the Turkish empire, and from various tribes and tongues. In a letter, dated in April, he says:

"The old depository in Stamboul has also sent increased supplies to the interior. I will mention one order for Kharput in Asia Minor, where Mr. Dunmore has recently been stationed.

182 Armenian Bibles and Testaments,
73 Psalms in Ancient and Modern Armenian,
32 Turkish Testaments and Psalms,
36 English Bibles and Testaments,
6 Italian Bibles,
18 Greek Bibles and Testaments,
12 Græco-Turkish Bibles and Testaments,
6 Armeno-Turkish Bibles,

---

365 Scriptures in different languages, and 1,462 various religious books, making together 1,828 volumes. Similar orders have likewise been received from Trebizond, Erzroom, Marsovan, and Tocat; all of which proves that the Word of God is beginning to run very swiftly through this land."

Under date of May 22 he writes:

" I have been attending the annual meeting of the Armenian Mission at Constantinople, during the last week, for the purpose of becoming acquainted with the missionaries from the interior, and enlisting their interest in the Bible Cause. They report an increased demand for the Scriptures at their various stations, and many interesting incidents of the great influence in some instances of even a single Bible or Testament in their fields of labor. I will mention one from the report of Rev. Mr. Clark, of Arabkir, respecting one of the stations in his field.

" ' The Turkish Governor of the city obtained from us a copy of the Scriptures, which he is said to read openly, and discuss its truths with Turks, Koords, and Armenians. And his banker, an Armenian, the teacher of the Armenian school, and some others petitioned us some time since to establish a regular Protestant service on the Sabbath.

" ' Light has also spread in the villages around and in the region beyond, among the wild Koords of the mountains. A copy of the New Testament which found its way into these wilds some four or five years since, having fallen into the hands of a Koordish chief, he has made it the law of his tribe. All matters are tried by the rules of the Gospel. Not only this, they seem to have received the Word in its spirit. They believe in Christ; have a kind of church organization, and celebrate the Lord's Supper in commemoration of his sufferings and death.'

"Mr. Clark also says: 'There is a large population in our field of Turks, called Ruzzel-bash. They seem to be a distinct party or tribe, and constitute the majority of Mussulmans in all this region. They are all ready to receive the Gospel; they believe in Christ; they observe not the great fast of the Mohammedans, neither do they use their forms of prayer, or practise their various washings. They pray extempore; they meet together once a year, make bread, and eat it, and say this is for Christ.

"'Two copies of the New Testament in Turkish, not long since, were carried to one of their villages. They were eagerly read and listened to. The villagers were amazed at the wonderful truths, and many joyfully received them. At length the villagers became divided among themselves, and many separated from their Mollah, and declared they would receive the truth at all hazards. And these men have already been subjected to much persecution for the Gospel's sake, one of them at the same time being the chief man of the village.

"'In another village, eight hours from Arabkir, a Ruzzel-bash has a Testament which he reads and preaches to his people; and he also is suffering much persecution. He is a Turk of some influence. 'It is the Lord's doing, and it is marvellous in our eyes.'"

"Thus are the Bible and the Gospel spreading among the Turks throughout the empire.

"We have received the following order for Scriptures from the Jewish station at Salonica: 100 Hebrew Bibles, 25 Spanish Bibles, 100 Hebrew Psalms, 100 Hebrew Pentateuch; indicating that a good work is also springing up amongst the Jews. And from Adrianople comes a call for 25 Turkish Testaments, and 80 Hebrew Psalms. May the Lord yet more abundantly bless His Word at all these stations, and in all these lands."

Some extracts are made from his correspondence, showing what an inviting field the camps and hospitals of the allied nations at Constantinople presented for the distribution of the Scriptures and how readily it was occupied.

"1,176 Bibles and Testaments have been sent to the English army in the Crimea. Lady Canning has generously purchased 200 Bibles and 500 Testaments, to be distributed among the British soldiers and sailors in the hospitals at Constantinople. Seventeen Russian prisoners have been supplied with Testaments. The visits of our colporteur were prevented for a time by authority of a sub-official who had charge of the prisoners; but he applied at once to Lord William Paulet, commander-in-chief of the forces of this station, and received the following order:

"'SCUTARI, March 31, 1855.

"'Mr. William Sellers has permission to have access to the Russian prisoners of war confined at the Turkish arsenal, for the purpose of supplying them with books.

"T. W. PAULET,
"B. General Com'g Troops.'"

The French soldiers seemed no less anxious than the English to obtain the Scriptures. He writes from Constantinople, May 22:

"The twenty thousand French soldiers encamped upon the heights above the Bosphorus, a few miles from the city, have furnished an interesting field for the distribution of the Scriptures during the last month. We had just begun fully to obtain access to them, however, as they were all ordered to the Crimea for the war; yet many will carry their little Testaments not only in the camp but also on the field of battle, and will find these their only consolation at the hour of death.

"I visited the camp a few days since, in company with a son of the Rev. Mr. Schauffler, for the purpose of obtaining a general authorization from the commander-in-chief, to distribute Bibles and Testaments among the soldiers. On the way we stopped at a shop of refreshments kept by a Protestant Armenian, where a few Testaments had previously been deposited, and inquired if he had any remaining on hand. 'Not one,' said he. 'Soon as the men found that New Testaments could be had here, they came and called earnestly for them, and my little supply was gone almost at once. I could distribute hundreds, if I gave them to all who wished. A commanding officer called here yesterday,' said he, 'and asked where these Testaments came from. I told him, a benevolent society had sent them.' He replied, 'Present my thanks to that society for so good a work.'

"This store, however, was not within the lines, and, according to camp regulation, the sentinels will allow no one to pass without a written order to that effect. And I wished a general permission for distributing the Bible to the soldiers in their tents, where a kind word might also be spoken accompanying the Word of Scripture.

"We called at head-quarters, but unfortunately found the General absent at Constantinople. On our return through the camp, however, we gained the following written permission from a colonel, stamped with his seal, freely to enter the lines of his regiment: '32d Regiment of Infantry. It is permitted to a colporteur, by the present permission, to circulate freely in the camp of the regiment, to bring there *works* for the use of the soldiers.'

" *Works* were of course interpreted to mean *Scriptures*, and we immediately sent a large supply of Testaments to his soldiers, who received them most gladly. While we were gone, two soldiers came from the hospital to the house of Mr. Schauffler, and begged for medicine and Testaments. One had previously received a Testament from there, and now he had brought his sick friend for one also; and as Mr. S. gave it to him, he said, with tears in his eyes, 'This is beyond all price to me. It will go with me till I die.' As there was yet one day before the troops were to embark, and the permission to visit one regiment susceptible of rather a general interpretation, we sent two colporteurs to enter the camp wherever this would admit them; and they thus distributed 300 Testaments to the soldiers, who manifested the greatest thankfulness at receiving them. Also, at the point of embarkation, on the following day, another was stationed to place in the hands of all whom he could reach at this last moment, the Word of Life, the way of everlasting salvation. Likewise, as they came from camp to Pera, a gratuitous supply was furnished them from our depository; and those who received Tes taments sent their friends for the same *bon livre*, and when others went to Bebek, there they received them by the roadside from the hands of Mr. Hamlin's little daughters, replying, with much gratitude, 'Merci, Mademoiselle, merci beaucoup, c'est bon"—Thank you, Miss, thank you much, it is good.

"More than a thousand Testaments have by these means, within a few days, been distributed to the troops. Thus, during their short encampment here, much good seed has been sown amongst them which we trust will not fail to spring up and bring forth fruit an hundredfold in the hearts of these poor soldiers, hurried away to die in a foreign land upon the field of battle. And we hope to gain still greater facilities for supplying with the same divine treasure the twenty-five thousand other troops now on their way from France to occupy this camp."

The seed thus sown will produce its fruit. Many of these soldiers died before leaving the Crimea, but many returned to France, bringing the Bible with them.

CHAPTER XI.

LETTERS HOME.

"CRIMEA, Dec. 25th, 1854.

"MY DEAR FATHER: I wish you 'merry, merry Christmas,' from the shores of the Black Sea. Here I am at the seat and centre of war, within the roar of the enemy's cannon, and in the midst of all the martial excitement and display of the camp, yet my thoughts and remembrance to-day fondly turn to those I love in the far off Western land. I am reminded of the many happy Christmas days I have spent at home, around our own fireside, and in our little family circle; I am reminded of the last we enjoyed together, when we were all gathered home and mingled in delightful social intercourse, my mind suddenly runs back through all the past years. I remember a father's kindness, tenderness and love, ever ready to grant my every wish and supply my every want; all this comes gushing up in mind to-day, and from the fulness of my heart I thank you for it all. None but he that feels it knows the gladness of such memories to a stranger in a strange land.

"But you will ask how I am spending Christmas here. First, we have excellent accommodations on board a transport ship in the harbor of Balaklava, the place of landing English stores for the army. We have roast goose, roast turkey, roast beef, and pork, for dinner, and right good cheer at the social table. As this is the first day (except Sabbath) that we have spent in the Crimea, we go up to Captain Frazer's battery upon the heights, above the town, to have a view of the camp—and it is indeed a brilliant scene. There are the Highland tents upon the highest hill; then a company of French Zouaves; then the Turks and English, and so on, for miles through the valleys; and along the hill-sides stretches the encampment, far as the eye can reach. At intervals the batteries are placed with sentinels to guard them, and a strong line of entrenchments the entire distance; and far in front are stationed the pickets on horseback, to give the alarm at the first approach of the enemy; just opposite, too, we see the Russian outposts, and they themselves, fifty thousand strong, are a few rods behind the hill. And here are foraging parties coming across the plain, French, Turks, and English, infantry and cavalry, on foot and on horseback, nobleman and commoner, prince and peasant, officers and soldiers alike mounted on horses, mules, donkeys, and dromedaries, driving carts, ambulance, and artillery wagons, bringing down the sick and marching up the new recruits; meeting and passing, shouting and hurrying each other forward; sticking fast in the mud and again moving on, all to the sound of martial music—fife, drum, and band. This forms the first picture, and gives us the first impression of all the pomp and circumstance of glorious war. But I must close. Farewell, dear Father.

"Your affectionate Son,

"CHESTER."

"CONSTANTINOPLE, Jan. 1, 1855.

"MY DEAR MOTHER: I wish you a happy New Year from the far East, my oriental home. The skies are bright and sunny here, and the air mild and genial, as I fondly trust they may be in the distant West, where 'the loved ones abide.' I have much enjoyed the day; in our American chapel we had a union meeting of Christians of every denomination in the city—the Evangelical Alliance of Constantinople. It was to me a delightful occasion, coming as I did directly from the seat and sound of war, and all the marshaling to arms and military excitement of the camp at Sebastopol, to enjoy this scene of peace here, where we met together in the name of the Prince of Peace, to hold sweet communion and fellowship with our Saviour and our God, and sit together in heavenly places in Christ Jesus. It was indeed good to be there, with our devoted Missionary friends and excellent English Christians, forgetting the distinctions of church and country, and becoming one in Christ Jesus our Lord. I was called upon to address the meeting, and though without preparation I felt strengthened in mind and spirit to give expression to the emotions which the time and place inspired. It seemed peculiarly appropriate to hold such a meeting at the opening of a new year, when the wheels of God's providence are rolling forward with mighty power in the East, preparing the way for the spread of the Bible, and preaching the Gospel of the ends of the world. This calls for renewed consecration to our Master's work at the beginning of the year. Another voice, too, spake to us in solemn tones. Just as the last year was coming to its close, the hand of death entered our little missionary circle, and suddenly took from us one who was beloved by all who knew her (Mrs. Everett), leaving a bereaved husband and tender sorrowing family to mourn her loss. The little children only whisper her name, 'Mamma's gone, mamma's gone to heaven!' Her voice spake to us that day, 'Be ye also ready, for in such an hour as ye think not, the Son of Man cometh.'"

"CONSTANTINOPLE, Feb. 4th, 1855.

MY DEAR MOTHER: In my last I wrote you of our Union meeting of English and American residents here, on New Year's day, which we all enjoyed so much in its spirit and influence. The next day was a full meeting of our Bible committee, which was of equal, if not greater interest to me. The next week there was also a meeting of all the Evangelical of the city, which I enjoyed very much; a Prussian presided, and the services were conducted in French, but there was one Lord and the same Spirit. There, too, we have such excellent preaching on the Sabbath in our American chapel, from all the good missionaries in their turn. They have kindly included me among their number, and I enjoy all, both the preaching and hearing, more than ever before. They are not only good men, but men of rare talent and ability at this station; and it is a delight and honor to be associated with them, and labor side by side with them in the same great cause. I likewise much enjoy our social family and singing meetings; they remind me of those we occasionally had at home, which linger still in mind with pleasantest memory. What is more delightful than the sound of familiar home-like music in a strange land?

"But I have just come from a meeting which has suggested to me this train of thought. It is the Sabbath, a mild and lovely day, and we have heard to-day a discourse on the occasion of the recent death of one of our missionary circle, the Rev. N. Benjamin. The text selected was from John xiv. 2, 3. 'In my Father's house are many mansions, if it were not so I would have told you. I go to prepare a place for you,' &c., and the subject was the preparation of the mansion for the disciple, and the disciple for the mansion. Both were done by Christ and through Christ. He was all, and in all, and above all, God blessed for ever. The preacher vividly portrayed the glory of the divinely-fitted mansion, and the still greater glory of the entrance of the redeemed soul within it, clothed with the righteousness and immortality of Christ. It was indeed a scene which every Christian should anticipate with rapture, and long to enjoy, desiring rather to depart and be with Christ, which is far better."

"CONSTANTINOPLE, April 29th, 1855.

"MY DEAR FATHER: It is the Sabbath, and my thoughts from this Moslem land are turned toward home, and those I love across the waters. Mingled with thoughts of home are likewise those of heaven, our home above, where I trust redeemed, purified, sanctified, glorified, in the image of Christ, we shall all meet in our Father's house, around his throne, where sin, sorrow, and sighing never enter, and parting shall be known no more for ever. This thought alone can sustain and cheer the soul, as separated from each other in distant lands we labor on, each in our own sphere, doing our appointed work, till our divine Master call us home, having overcome, 'to sit down with Him on his throne, even as He also overcame, and is set down with his Father on his throne.'

"My meditations were divided thus as I sat down to write you this afternoon, and also such thoughts and questions as these passed through my mind. Winter has passed, and gladsome spring has come—the season of life, and bloom, and beauty. How have father and mother enjoyed the winter? how are they at this returning spring? True, I have their open portraits before me, with lineaments and feature unchanged since I left (which I value above price); yet these are not sufficient to satisfy the fulness of the heart. I would know more. Have they grown old at all since I have gone? have the infirmities of age begun to gather upon them? Oh, that I could visit home but for one short hour, to see and speak a word with each, and feel assured that all were well as when I left; I could then return and press forward in earnest duty, with a firmer step and warmer heart. But why should I distrust? Do I not daily commend them all to the guardian care and loving kindness of Him who is Omnipotent and Omnipresent, who doeth all things well, and whose tender mercies are over all his works.

* * * * * * * * *

CHAPTER XII.

VISIT TO A RUINED CITY.

THE following interesting account of a ruined city was sent to the "New York Observer" with which he corresponded from the East.

"BROOSA, June 27th, 1855.

"MESSRS. EDITORS: In company with the Rev. Dr. Hamlin, I came yesterday to visit Broosa, the scene of the recent earthquake in the Orient. We left Constantinople in the early morning, on board of a Turkish steamer, and sailed out upon the Sea of Marmora, past the Princes Isles, and coasting along the shores of Asia, crowned with cypresses, myrtles, and pines, in six hours we came to Moudania, a small Greek town on the Gulf of Nicea. Here we landed, and took horses for a ride of six hours more in the interior. Our horses were equipped in the oriental style. Mine was mounted with a saddle of blue cloth, and wore a band of colored beads, and cloth worked with sea-shells about his neck, and dangling brass ornaments upon his bridle.

"Upon leaving the town, we rode a short distance along the water-side, and then through the rich vineyards and olive groves of the country. Ascending the hill, we had a lovely view of the valley before us, covered with green pasturage, and fields of ripened grain ready for the sickle. Wild flowers, the woodbine, blue bell, and hollyhock, were in bloom beside our path, and the hum of locusts, and singing of birds filled the air with music. We crossed a small ravine, and came to another summit that commanded a still more extended and picturesque view. We looked over the whole plain of Broosa, twenty miles in length, cultivated with wheat fields, the olive, mulberry, and the grape. The river Ulfar wound its way in the centre, and herds of cattle and flocks of sheep were feeding by the river side. Shepherds were attending these, and the reapers were in the fields, gathering their grain. In the distance 'the minareted city' rose before us on the mountain slope, and Mount Olympus towered above, piercing the clouds: the whole combining the grand and beautiful with most impressive effect. Descending upon the plain, we forded the river, and refreshed ourselves at a small caffee station under two large oak trees. It was most pleasant to receive the good-natured salutations of the Turks,—Rhosh gueldiniz, safa gueldiniz, chelibi: 'You are welcome, very welcome, gentlemen,'—

at each stopping-place, and by the roadside as we passed, indicating a remarkably favorable change of feeling toward the giaours in these latter days.

"As we proceeded on our way, suddenly a dark cloud rose from behind Mount Olympus, and came advancing toward the plain. The lightning flashed from it, and the thunder rolled fearfully down the mountain side. It drew near, and the rain and hail came like falling columns upon us. Our horses whirled round and trembled with fear, and we knew not but another earthquake was just at hand, so great was the commotion of the elements. Yet the scene was one of the sublimest in nature, filling the mind with awe. The storm continued only a few minutes, and sweet indeed was the sunshine, 'when 'twas past.' It diffused, too, a delightful coolness in the air, and cleansed and purified the face of the landscape. The approach to Broosa, under these circumstances, was exceedingly beautiful, as the clear sunlight was gilding the shattered minarets, domes, and towers, and painting the rainbow upon the dark background of cloud that passed behind the city.

"We began to see the effects of the earthquake immediately upon entering the suburbs. The plaster was shaken from the sides of the houses, the tiles and timbers from the roofs, the walls were cracked. Some buildings were entirely thrown down in a mass, the domes of the mosques were crushed in, the tops of the minarets broken off, and piles of stone and rubbish filled the streets. Here, huge boulders came tumbling down the mountain, and crushed everything before them, and a little beyond, we passed by the ruins of a large silk factory, where forty girls were buried in the fall, and some of them crushed instantly to death by one of these large masses of rock rolling through the building, though others lived for several hours, screaming for help. Their bodies are still lying under the heaps of rubbish. The terrified inhabitants fled from the earthquake at once upon the plain, but after the first shocks had passed, returned to the city, and gathered materials to build huts and tents for safety, entirely deserting their shattered houses. They had just begun to return and repair them, however, when a second earthquake came upon them, more destructive than the first, laying waste the city, and forcing them to flee again for temporary protection to their huts and tents. They have now begun to return a second time and prop up their houses, and build little wooden stalls for trading, and some are erecting new residences. The silk factories, most of which were but slightly injured, have commenced operation, and quite a new spirit of activity and enterprise is springing up in the city. Yet they all live in constant dread of another shock without a moment's warning.

"It was sad indeed, as we wound through the streets, to see such marks of ruin and desolation on every hand. We arrived at the house of a Protestant Armenian, just as the sun was setting and flooding the sky with golden glory. How delightful it is to receive the cordial welcome of a friend in a strange land, and that too from the hand of a stranger, when a spirit of Christian love fills the heart.

"We came drenched with wet and exhausted by our journey. They at once provided us with dry clothing, a neat room, and a *mangal* of coals in the centre; sent a servant with a basin of warm water to wash and rub our feet, as is the oriental custom; gave us Armenian cloaks lined with fur, to prevent our taking cold by the exposure; prepared us an excellent supper from the well-cooked dishes of the country; brought pipes and tobacco for a soothing influence, and then sat down and talked, till a late hour in the evening, of the Gospel and the love of Christ. I remarked:

"'This was far greater kindness than I ever expected from a stranger, far in the interior of Turkey.'

"'Oh,' said they, 'when our benefactors from America come to visit us, we love to express to them the fulness of our gratitude for sending us the Bible and the Gospel of salvation. We pray you to receive it all as coming from our heart.'

"I said to them, 'It seemed like Bunyan's Pilgrim at the palace called Beautiful, who was received and entertained simply because his name was Christian.'

"We too slept in 'the chamber of Peace,' and awoke to sing hymns of praise and thanksgiving to our Lord and Saviour.

"In the morning, after accomplishing my official business, I set out to explore the ruins of the city. First I visited several of the old khans or large public buildings, with an open court in the centre, let to merchants and travellers. These were all filled with ruins, so that it was quite impossible to occupy them. Then I came to the Mosque of Sultan Bajazid, the largest in the empire. Its principal walls are still standing. I readily obtained admission by giving a backshish to the keeper of the keys. The architectural effect of the immense columns, and the twenty-four domes supporting the roof, and the sense of vastness within, surpasses any of the mosques I have visited at Constantinople. It is adorned with inscriptions in golden letters from the Koran on the walls, and the high altar is elaborately wrought and gilded in the arabesque style. A fountain is still playing in the centre, though the domes are so much shattered and crushed, that it is not used for Moslem worship. Through some I could see the clouds passing, and the clear blue sky above. It seemed dangerous to remain long, as the least agitation would have precipitated the broken cornices and columns upon us. I therefore hastened out, when an old Turk stepped up to me at the door, and asked with an air of great satisfaction:

"'Well, Chelibi, have you any such great buildings as this in your country, where you came from?'

"I said, 'Yes, this was very grand, but the Franks had Cathedrals much more splendid.'

"At which he expressed much surprise and said, Allah mashallah, 'God is merciful,' and walked away.

"I then with much difficulty gained permission to ascend one of the minarets and take a view of the city, perhaps the first time this was ever granted to a European. The Moslems guard their minarets with special care, and allow none but Muezzims, or criers to prayer, to climb them, and these are often selected from among the blind, lest they should see any of their women unveiled as they walk out into the private gardens. The panorama around was beautiful beyond description. Mount Olympus towered above in rugged grandeur; Broosa, with its khans and mosques, its fountains, factories, and palaces, partly in ruins, partly active with life, stretched along the mountain side; and beyond lay the lovely plain, planted with the mulberry, walnut, and oak, and cultivated with fruitful vineyards and fields of corn and wheat, rejoicing in luxuriant beauty; while the whole, like an amphitheatre, was encircled by a chain of hills, which circumscribed and fixed limits to the view that the mind might fully comprehend and enjoy the scene.

"Descending thence we took a cavass, and visited the mosque of the celebrated Sultan Orkhan, who conquered Broosa in 1326. It is splendidly built of white marble, and ornamented with much carving on the outside walls. The interior is decorated with Persian porcelain of variegated colors, and the Mirah curiously wrought in antique style. At a side altar are two large copies of the Koran in golden letters, executed with much artistic effect. We also entered the Salamlik, or Sultan's station for performing prayers, apart from and above the rest. This was richly finished with porcelain and gold, and beside it was another closely latticed, for the Sultana to join in her prayers at the same time; the first of the kind I have seen in any mosque. He must have had a higher regard for the sex than the Turks generally. The whole is so shattered by the earthquake as to be rendered unfit for use. The same is also true of all the three hundred and sixty-five mosques of the city; not one of them is entered by Mussulmen for prayer; a severe blow, indeed, to their religion. They regard their places of worship with most devout reverence, resorting to them five times a day to repeat their prayers. And now the curse of Allah rests upon them.

"We then went to the tomb of the Sultan, a marble mausoleum, in which he and six of his family are buried. It is situated in a large court filled with shade and fruit trees, and built with much magnificence, but it is also tottering upon its base, and just ready to fall and bury them again deep in the ruins. The great conqueror has selected a lovely spot for his last resting-place,—at the base of Mount Olympus, enshrined in sculptured marble, surrounded by wide-spreading shade trees, and overlooking the charming plain of Broosa. We then descended from this elevated point of table land, and threading our way through the dilapidated streets, came to Daoud Monastery, once an ancient Greek church, but subsequently converted into a mosque. In proof of which we saw a cross of colored marble worked into one of the columns, and another carved with the chisel upon a capital. Here Osman, the founder of the Ottoman empire, lies buried. The whole is one mass of broken ruins. The earthquake at this point seems to have spent its greatest force. Solid marbles and granites have been rent asunder by the shock, like cords of tow, and thrown together in confused heaps. Never before have I seen such broken fragments. Our cavass now gave us a description of its effect. Said he:

"'There was first a deep, rumbling noise and a loud explosion upwards, and then the whole mountain and earth surged to and fro and trembled as if shaken by the wind. The shocks continued all night. The buildings were falling on all sides, and the women and children shrieked, and fled in every direction for safety. It was a scene terrific beyond conception.'

"We then ascended to the castle hill, and took a last view of the city and country around. This point in front marks the track of the great rocks that were precipitated from the mountain-side, and spread desolation in their path to the plain; there on the right the flames burst forth and laid waste a whole district of the city, and we saw marks of destruction on every hand, though much that was beautiful still rose above the ruins. On the left were several large silk factories, apparently quite uninjured, and we descended through the old castle gate to visit one of these establishments. I was much surprised to find it worked entirely by steam and machinery, attended by factory girls, well dressed, and exhibiting all the enterprise and activity of a Lowell or Lawrence mill. We learned there were twenty-four factories in the city, and only two or three were destroyed by the earthquake. The remainder are now in active operation. Indeed, these and the silk-growing business, form the only dependence of the people.

"We then rode through the Olympian valley, thickly overgrown with vines, and watered by a mountain stream, and around the walls of Castle Hill, built in the massive Byzantine style, and came to an old burial-ground deeply shaded with cypresses and venerable trees. The tombs were ornamented with large turbans and swords, and some with the round crowned hats of Dervishes, telling both of the warlike and fanatical spirit of those olden times. Passing this, and winding through the ruined streets, we at length arrived at the house of our Protestant friend, Baron Bedros. After an excellent dinner in native style, I bid the family a friendly farewell, and received also their cordial salaams at parting, and then set out on my return journey, accompanied only by a Surigi, or Turkish guide, to lead the way. We came down directly upon the plain, and passed along a well-shaded road, through thousands of acres of mulberry trees, and fields of corn and wheat, and pasturage for cattle. At length we reached a village entirely destroyed by the earthquake and deserted by its inhabitants. A large number of storks, however, had taken possession, and built their nests among the ruins. Here I am joined by a Turk as travelling companion, and we gallop together on our way. The road is well made and in sections paved or macadamised, but there are no bridges, and we must ford all the streams, some of which are deep and dangerous. There are caffee stations every few miles, at which it is the custom of the country to stop and refresh with coffee and chibouques. But this was not sufficient for my Turkish friend. He carried his long pipe with him, and filled it, and smoked on horseback as we rode along, which seemed to me decidedly the pursuit of pleasure under difficulties. We climbed up the hill-side and enjoyed a combined view of the mountain, city, and plain on the one side, and a valley of vineyards, olive groves and fig trees stretching to the sea on the other, while the clear sunlight was resting on the whole landscape, like a picture before us. It was a scene of beauty I shall long remember. The old Turk exclaimed, 'Guzel tchok, guzel chelibi,' 'Pretty, very pretty, sir!' and drew a long puff from his pipe with peculiar delight that this was the land of the Moslems. Descending thence along a winding road, in two hours we reached Gimleck, and set sail on board the Turkish steamer again for Constantinople.

"Sincerely yours,

"C. N. R."

CHAPTER XIII.

VISIT TO GREECE.

IT was the intention of Mr. Righter on leaving the United States to visit Greece, on his way to the East, for the purpose of ascertaining the condition of that country in respect to the Bible, and to prepare the way for its supply. But, as has been already mentioned, on reaching Malta, he determined to defer his visit on account of the prevalence of the cholera at Athens, and because he had acquired much of the information that he desired. This visit he made the next fall, leaving Constantinople for Athens, October 1, 1855.

In a letter to the Secretary of the American Bible Society, he gives the following account of his voyage and his visit at Athens:

"ATHENS, October 20, 1855.

"MY DEAR FRIEND:—Feeling that I had too long neglected Greece, in consequence of the superior importance of Constantinople as a centre of operations, I determined on the 1st of October to make a short visit to Athens, in behalf of the

Bible cause. On my way I called at Smyrna, while our steamer was remaining a few hours in port. I found the work there going forward with increasing interest. Three dépôts are established for the sale and distribution of the Scriptures: the mission depository in a large square opposite the great mosque of the city—they sell many Arabic Bibles to caravans from the interior, and have much demand for the Armeno-Turkish Testament: the depot of the Church Missionary Society, under the direction of the Rev. Mr. Walters, in the business part of the town—they sell many Turkish, Modern Greek, and Græco-Turkish Scriptures: and the depot of the British and Foreign Bible Society, containing Bibles and Testaments in all the languages of the East, and used as a magazine for supplying the interior stations. In addition to these agencies it is thought that a colporteur is much needed to supply the sailors in the port, and to sell and distribute the Scriptures from house to house.

"A private gentleman, Mr. Richard Van Lennep, has recently had printed 1,000 copies of the Gospel of John, in Greek with Roman characters, for the benefit of the islanders who speak the Greek, but do not understand the Greek letters. More than 200 of these have already been circulated at his own expense. I also learned an interesting incident with regard to the Bible, at ancient

Thyatira, one of the seven churches of Asia, where a new Evangelical church has lately been organized. Considerable opposition was excited against the Protestants on the part of some bigoted Greeks, and they devised the following plan at once to crush the infant church. They sent to Smyrna, and bought a large Bible, and presented it to a Turk, the chief man of the village, that he might publicly condemn the book in which the Protestants believed. He began to read in the New Testament, and instead of finding anything to condemn, pronounced it all good. He became more and more interested, and invited a number of Turks to listen to the reading of the Gospel. All gave it their approbation, and the Christians were triumphantly sustained. It is hoped that a good work may spring up among the Turks there, through the defeat of this wicked device of the Evil One.

"Thence I proceeded on the voyage to Athens. We were unfortunately detained six days in quarantine, at the Piræus, as a case of cholera was reported to have occurred at Smyrna, while our steamer was lying in the harbor.

"Immediately after my arrival in the city I called upon Dr. King, and had a full interview with him in regard to the Athens edition of the modern Greek Testament, and the prospects of the Bible Cause in Greece. He informs me that the edition is very well received, though the style is somewhat elevated for the common people in the country.

"Dr. King considers it a most favorable time, at present, to make a new effort in distributing the Bible among the Greeks. The bishops and priests have lost their old prejudice against the Scriptures, the government are entirely well disposed, and the people ready to receive the Word of Life. He has a class of eight theological students, devoted, pious young men; four of whom are anxious to spend their vacation as colporteurs, travelling in Macedonia, Thessaly, and Albania, to sell and distribute the Bible. This seemed to me a most excellent enterprise, but I did not feel authorized to warrant the expense of three or four hundred dollars, without first referring the matter to our Committee at New York. Also, the doctor is very desirous that a new Bible and Religious Book Depository be opened in the central street of the city, on the plan of that at Constantinople, which would also be a centre of religious influence and discussion. This likewise meets with my cordial approbation, and I would at once refer the question to our Board, whether they are disposed to sustain their proportion of the expense of such a depository at Athens. The whole expense of the establishment is estimated at $500 per year.

"I also visited the small dépôt which Dr. King has under his charge, at his own house. He has sold and distributed from thence during the last year 368 Bibles and Testaments. I was quite astonished at the number of Scriptures that have been circulated in Greece, through Dr. King's instrumentality, since his residence in the country: They amount to an average of three or four thousand each year, for a period of twenty-five years, making between 75,000 and 100,000 copies, that have thus gone forth through all the land, in their mission of mercy and love.

"I also held a conference with the Rev. Dr. Hill, in relation to the Bible interests. His views agreed substantially with those of Dr. King, with regard to the Athens edition of the New Testament, and the favorable prospects for the distribution of the Scriptures at present. He said he knew that 'five, at least, of the archbishops and bishops of the Greek church were favorable to the circulation of the Bible among their people, and the government were quite ready to have the Testament introduced and taught in all their schools.'

"Dr. Hill kindly gave me an introduction to the Director of Public Schools, who expressed an earnest desire to have their schools supplied with the New Testament. He stated that there were 550 government schools in Greece—400 for boys, and 150 for girls, embracing 40,000 children; and if we gave ten Testaments to each school, they would consequently need 5,500 copies to meet the demand. Dr. Hill, who was present, at once offered to superintend the distribution of whatever number I might choose to designate for that purpose. I then called upon Mr. Nicholaides, the Agent of the British and Foreign Bible Society at Athens, under whose direction the new edition of the Testament was published. I stated to him the arrangement I had previously made with the officers of that society, in London, that the books should be printed expressly for us, and sold to us at cost price. He informed me that 5,000 had been published, and 2,000 were already disposed of, so that 3,000 only remained on hand. Of these, I have ordered that 1,000 be placed in the government schools, and 300 in the school under the direction of Mrs. Hill. He states that a second edition of 5,000 copies can be published here, if desired, in three or four months.

"I was much interested in a visit I made to Mrs. Hill's mission school. She has under her charge between three and four hundred Greek girls and children. They are regularly and thoroughly taught in the Scriptures. Indeed, I was quite surprised at the promptness and entire accuracy of their answers to Bible questions. She desired 400 New Testaments and 100 Bibles for her school. Dr. and Mrs. Hill have been engaged in this mission for more than twenty years, and have done a noble work in the religious education of the daughters of Greece. They are now reaping the reward of their labors, in seeing their pupils occupying positions of honor and usefulness in all the land. I also visited, in company with Dr. Hill, the government schools of Athens, for the purpose of ascertaining whether the Scriptures were taught, and if they desired a further supply. The first we visited was a school for boys, numbering 450, conducted on the Lancasterian principle. The New Testament, Evangelia, is introduced into the regular course of instruction, and taught morning and evening. I said to the principal, that 'we in America were much interested in the Greeks, especially in the schools of Greece, and were desirous to furnish them with the Bible as the basis of all true education.'

"'I am well aware of this,' said he; 'the Americans have always done us good, and we feel particularly grateful to you for the Bible.' I was much pleased with the order and efficiency of their system, and the bright, intelligent countenances of the boys. He requested me to send him twenty-five or thirty New Testaments for his school.

"Then we made a visit to a government school for girls, situated in the ancient Agora, where St.

Paul preached. This numbered 350, under the superintendence of an excellent lady, and was most admirably conducted. It was truly cheering to know that they were all instructed in the Word of God, and taught the way of everlasting life. One of the teachers remarked to me that 'their Scriptures were quite exhausted, and they much needed a new supply.'

"We then visited the Normal School for the education of teachers. The instruction here is given by lectures from professors, and one lecture a week is devoted to the Bible. One of the professors spoke English very well, and said to me: 'You must be very much encouraged by your visit. The Scriptures now have free circulation in Greece. All that we need is a full supply.'

"The university, also, which numbers 650 students, has a course of lectures in Biblical theology. Indeed, a far more liberal and evangelical spirit now prevails in Greece, and it seems a most favorable moment to commence new operations for placing the Scriptures in their schools, and distributing them throughout the country. This is the only hope for the future of this ancient classic land. I was much encouraged by the kind and friendly manner in which I was received by all in behalf of the Bible Cause.

"Having thus fully accomplished the object of

my visit, I determined at once to return again to Constantinople.

"Most sincerely your friend and brother,

"C. N. RIGHTER."

He gives, in his correspondence, the following account of a Sabbath at Athens:

"ATHENS, Oct. 14, 1855.

"In the morning early, I went, in company with a friend, to attend the services of the Greek church. The first we entered was very small and humble in appearance, designed for the poorer classes, yet it was fully attended. They seemed very degraded and bigoted in the observance of form, devoutly kissing the pictures of the Virgin and saints, and pressing them with their foreheads, holding lighted candles, and crossing themselves incessantly. Their worship is very like that of the Romish church, consisting of reading the liturgy, and nasal singing by priests and small boys, burning incense, swinging the censer, and various outward rites. They have the lower forms of the Roman Catholics without their soul-inspiring music and splendid cathedrals.

"We then sought out the large church of St. Irene, in the central street of the city. This is principally attended by the higher classes. It is massive and finely built, though still unfinished.

A high gallery above is assigned to the ladies. The paintings of the Trinity and saints were conspicuous above the high altar. The service was similar to the former on a more elevated scale. The priests and bishops were engaged in consecrating three loaves of bread, by burning lighted candles, and swinging incense over them. This was afterwards passed around and received as the body of Christ by the multitude. Such is the superstitious ceremony and observance of the Greek church.

"I then went to attend the Protestant Greek service at Dr. King's chapel, which is built upon his own grounds, and has recently been opened, after being closed for a period of seven years. The audience consisted of forty or fifty persons, assembled to enjoy the worship of God in spirit and in truth. Though it was a strange language in a land of strangers, yet it was delightful to feel that there was the same spirit of faith and love to Christ our common Saviour. The Doctor took for his text these solemn words: 'To-day, if ye will hear his voice, harden not your hearts.' His manner was earnest and eloquent, and the truth reached the hearts of his hearers. Never did I see a more attentive congregation. Every eye was directed upon the speaker throughout the discourse, as though all were listening for their lives.

"And much, indeed, did I enjoy this scene and influence of spiritual worship in contrast with what I had just witnessed of dead and soulless formality. Dr. King is greatly encouraged in his labors at present, so that he cannot feel it his duty to return home while such a work is springing up around him, though he spoke with tears in his eyes of his desire to go out and gather his separated children in one family, that he might give them a father's counsel, and blessing, and die in peace.

"He has a class of eight Greek students in theology, sent to his house, and supported by the Western Asia Missions' Aid Society. To them he delivers three lectures a week on biblical interpretation and systematic theology. They are thus abundantly qualified for religious discussion, and to exert a favorable influence upon all with whom they come in contact. Indeed, it seems a remarkable providence that has brought them here just at this time. I have no doubt but it is the dawning of a better day for Greece.

"He is not molested at all in his work, but, through faith and perseverance, has overcome every form of persecution. A Greek priest came to him a few days since, and said, 'I believe you preach the truth. We must return to the Bible.' The lawyer who was engaged on his trial has become his warm friend, and the government is no longer hostile. The truth of his life and preaching has thus triumphed over all opposition. Great, indeed, must be his joy in living to see these fruits of his labors, and reap the reward of his faithfulness and devotion in the service of his Divine Master. 'Be not weary in well-doing; for in due season ye shall reap, if ye faint not.'

"In the afternoon I went out with my Bible in my hand, and ascending the steps cut in the solid rock, stood upon 'Mars Hill,' where Paul preached eighteen hundred years ago, and there read the sublime discourse of the Apostle 'to the men of Athens,' wherein he set forth to them the Unknown God, whom they ignorantly worshipped, and declared to them that the Maker of heaven and earth dwelleth not in temples made with hands, neither is the Godhead like unto gold, or silver, or stone graven by art and man's device, for we are his offspring: in Him we live, and move, and have our being.

"Standing here upon the very rock where he stood, and in sight of the ruined temples to which he then referred in all their magnificence and beauty, I realized as never before the boldness and impressive eloquence of the great Apostle to the Gentiles. Around him was the high court of the Areopagus, the Epicurean and Stoic philosophers, and the idle crowd that had followed him from the Agora to hear what 'this babbler would say.' Before him were the altars of many gods, goddesses, and heroes of Pagan mythology, and above him rose the Acropolis, crowned with marble temples, and devoted to heathen worship, and filled with statues and idols of gold, silver, and stone, exhibiting all the refined art of Greece in the days of her proudest glory. And in the midst of all Paul stood up and preached to them Jesus and the resurrection, repentance and judgment to come, while 'some mocked, and others said, we will hear thee again of this matter.' As I stood alone amid the memory of such scenes as this, and saw around me these splendid ruins of human greatness and power, I felt that God only was great, and man and his works were mortal and perishing. I felt, too, the truth of the same resurrection that Paul preached, and our need of the same Jesus that he declared, to deliver us from death and the grave, and clothe us with immortal life.

"I remained long in contemplating the scene and holding communion with the invisible God, and then returned at evening through the crowded streets of the city to my room, filled with impressions of the Sabbath that will never be forgotten.

"The following Sabbath we attended church at the English chapel connected with the British embassy. The Rev. Dr. Hill performed the service, and delivered a very excellent discourse from the words of Paul, 'I press toward the mark for the prize of the high calling of God in Christ Jesus.'

"It was indeed most cheering and encouraging to the Christian heart far from home, thus to join with the people of God in his house of prayer, and sit together in heavenly places in Christ Jesus. In the evening I was invited to be present at the religious exercises of Dr. Hill's school. The smaller girls were first assembled, and Scripture exposition, singing and prayer conducted in Greek. Then the older pupils were gathered in the parlor, and their devotions held in English. I was much interested to see these Greek girls listening with earnestness to the reading of the gospel and the words of exhortation the Dr. addressed to them, then joining in singing an evening hymn of praise, and all bowing in prayer and thanksgiving to the Father of Mercies, from whom cometh down every good and perfect gift.

"The school at present numbers between three and four hundred Greek girls and children, under the efficient and systematic direction of Mrs. Hill. It has been in operation more than twenty years, and has exerted a wide and lasting influence upon the educational and spiritual interests of Greece.

"Through such agencies as these at work, and

the Scriptures introduced and taught in all the government and public schools, there is much hope for the future of this ancient classic land.

"Most sincerely yours,

"C. N. R."

CHAPTER XIV.

VISIT TO EGYPT.

AFTER completing the object of his visit to Athens, Mr. Righter returned to Constantinople, reaching the latter place Oct. 30th. He resumed his labors here with the same earnestness with which he had pursued them before his departure; and, having made arrangements for the prosecution of the work of Bible distribution during his absence, with the advice of friends who were interested in the cause, he determined upon making a journey to Egypt and the Holy Land, to inquire into the condition of those countries with reference to the Word of Life, and to provide for the supply of their destitution as far as it could be done. Accordingly, having all things ready, he took his departure again from Constantinople Dec. 27th, on board the steamer Emily, bound for Alexandria. The account of his voyage is given in his own words.

"In company with an American friend, I set sail from the Golden Horn just as the sunset was gilding the domes, minarets, and palaces of Constantinople. On our right was the wide-reaching Bosphorus, lined with kiosks and country seats, stretching far to the Black Sea; on the left, the Golden Horn, spanned with bridges, and filled with the shipping of all nations, winding to the valley of sweet waters; before us was Pera, the chosen residence of Franks, crowned with the Russian, French, and English palaces; on one side was Stamboul, the old Turkish city, crowned with mosques, minarets, and monuments, and fronted by the Seraglio Palace, the proud home of the ancient Sultans, ornamented with gardens and evergreen shade trees; and just opposite, Scutari, in Asia, overlooked by its immense military hospital, and forest cemetery of cypress; and the Princess Isles beyond, standing out in the sea of Marmora, as a citadel to guard the entrance to all of these.

"We sailed all night across the Sea of Marmora, and in the morning were passing through the Dardanelles, with the shores of Europe and Asia on either side. We glided by the modern castles of Europe and Asia, and the ancient Sestos and Abydos, where Leander was wont to swim the Straits to visit his Hero; and came to the ruins of old Troy, on the shore, and the island of Tenedos, near by, and on past the picturesque shores of Mytilene, the landing-place of the Apostle

Paul on his voyage to Athens, and cast anchor for the night in the broad and beautiful harbor of Smyrna.

"The next day was the Sabbath. We called upon the Rev. Mr. Ladd, American Missionary, and attended his Turkish service at the chapel in the morning. Though the language is a strange tongue, yet the gospel always sounds delightful to a Christian traveller in a strange land. A little congregation of the natives, Armenians, Greeks, and Jews, were assembled, and listened to the earnest discourse of the preacher with marked attention. It is pleasing to find the good work prospering here under the faithful labors of our missionaries; and Armenians, Greeks, and Mussulmans receiving the Bible and the faith of Christ in simplicity and in truth, thus rekindling anew the pure light of the gospel in the ancient church of Asia, which had centuries since gone out in darkness, whose golden candlestick has long been removed out of its place.

"The next morning, accompanied by the Rev. Mr. Morgan, we visited the old Greek Church where the Bishop Polycarp is said to have preached. Over the door, I read the inscription in ancient characters, POLYCARPION SE THEION POMENA (Polycarp the divine shepherd). It is elegantly decorated within, and nine silver lamps are kept burning night and day. A large screen stands before the high altar, elaborately carved in oak, representing all the various scenes in the New Testament, connected with the birth, life, death, and resurrection of Christ,—the work of many years of diligent labor, all cut by the hands of one who was deaf and dumb. Then we mounted to the old Genoese castle upon the hill, which commands a view of the city, harbor, mountains, and country round. Here, underneath a tall cypress tree, stands the tomb of the good Bishop Polycarp, and near by is the amphitheatre where he suffered martyrdom for the witness of Jesus and the Word of God. How inspiring it is to the Christian faith to visit such a spot sealed by the blood of one who bore such testimony to the truth as it is in Jesus. When called upon by the slaves of the Roman Emperor to curse Christ and do sacrifice, he replied, 'Eighty and six years I have served him, and he has done me nothing but good; how can I curse my Lord and Saviour?' Then he freely gave himself up to his persecutors to kindle the flames around him. Mussulmen now come up to this place every year to offer their sacrifice of sheep at the great festival of Bairam. Within the bounds of the amphitheatre we saw the caverns whence the wild beasts were let loose upon the Christians in the arena, to tear them limb from limb, and we could distinctly trace the outline of the seats where the Pagan multitude assembled to witness this bloody spectacle.

"From a ruined tower of the Castle we enjoyed a lovely panoramic view of the villages, valleys, and surrounding country of Asia Minor. Here is the site of ancient Smyrna, the Crown of the East, and near by the River Mylis flows to the sea, on whose banks the ancients claimed that Homer was born; beyond lie the valley and River Hermes, celebrated in classic song, and the broad Mediterranean stretches far in the distance —all spread out like a picture before us. From this point, too, we could trace distinctly the location of the seven churches of Asia, in the precise order in which they are mentioned in the Revelations: Ephesus, Smyrna, Pergamos, Thyatira, Sardis, Philadelphia, and Laodicea, whose ruined sites still remain to attest the truth of Scripture, and the terrible fulfilment of the prophecy of 'Him that liveth and was dead, and is alive for evermore.' Descending thence we visited a large Armenian church in the centre of the city. It was newly built, and contained a painting of the Trinity, the Father, Son, and Holy Spirit, and the single Eye of Omniscience over all, to guard the purity of his house and worship, much fitted to impress the ignorant and bigoted multitude.

"On the following day we embarked again on board our steamer for Alexandria, and in the evening passed the celebrated Island of Scio, another reputed birth-place of the great poet, Homer.

> "'Seven cities claimed the birth of Homer dead,
> Through which the living Homer begged his bread.'

"Then come Nikaros and Samos, just beyond, and now we sail among

> "'The Isles of Greece, the Isles of Greece,
> Where burning Sappho loved and sung,
> Where grew the arts of war and peace,—
> Where Delos rose, and Phœbus sprung,
> Eternal summer gilds them yet,
> And all except their sun is set.'

Here is Tinos and Delos, Coos, Naxos and Paros, all famed in classic history and poetry. The morning sun rises over the isle of Patmos in the distance, and in two hours more we are passing just beside it. With a good glass I could discern the houses in the village, and the convent that marks the place where the beloved disciple received the sublime revelations of the Apocalypse. It indeed filled the mind with sacred emotions to feel that we were gazing upon the precise spot where angels and the Saviour himself descended to reveal 'the things which must shortly come to pass.' Here also a door was opened in heaven, and the future glories of the spiritual world, the golden streets of the New Jerusalem, the City of our God, the great white throne and Him that sat upon it, whose face was to look upon like a jasper and a sardine stone, and cherubim and seraphim, and a multitude that no man can number, out of every kindred, and tongue, and people, and nation, with palms in their hands, clothed in white robes, washed and made pure in the blood of the Lamb, were all made to pass in heavenly vision before the mind of the inspired prophet. I took my Bible, and read again and again these divine scenes, and realized as never before their full and glorious truth and power.

"At evening we enjoyed a gorgeous sunset in the sea, such as one rarely sees, even in the orient, as if to give effect to the impressions of the day, ever changing ever new, such as no artist can pencil. Rising just above the horizon yonder, Patmos seems floating in the distance, like an island of the blest. Two days more of sailing in the open sea brought us safely to our destined port, Alexandria.

"At Alexandria I called upon the Rev. Mr. Brown, missionary of the Free Church of Scotland, and conferred with him in reference to the interests of the Bible Cause. He informed me that there was no Bible dépôt established in the city, and until recently very little had been accomplished in circulating the Scriptures. Within the last three months, however, a zealous young man from Beyrout, Mr. Spillman, had labored with much success as Bible colporteur, selling the Scriptures in the streets, from house to house, and among the shipping of all nations in the harbor. Mr. Spillman gave me the following list of Scriptures he has thus sold in twelve different languages: 27 Arabic, 39 Italian, 25 Greek, 8 French, 6 Hebrew, 4 Turkish, 6 English, 2 Swedish, 2 Coptic, 2 Armenian, 2 German, 1 Danish; making together 124 copies, for 960 piastres. He has also the encouragement that his labors are attended with immediate good results. He related to me, among others, the following interesting incident: A Greek of Damascus, living at Alexandria, became convinced, by reading the Bible, of the errors of his church and the truth of the Protestant faith. He immediately began to instruct others, and through his influence six were persuaded to renounce the Greek religion. They suffered much persecution from the bigoted Greeks, and one night, while at their devotions, they were attacked by a party of forty or fifty, armed with knives and sticks, but were delivered from their hands by the Turkish police. He has since sold eight Bibles in that very room; one of the first persecutors has himself become a devout believer, and now a goodly number assemble there to read the Scriptures together, and have prayers in the name of Jesus Christ. Through the humble labors of this one colporteur, so much interest is beginning to be manifested in the Bible work, that Mr. Brown thought the time had already come for opening a Bible depository in the central street of the city, similar to that established at Constantinople, which would bring the Scriptures in every language publicly before the notice of all, and thus greatly increase their sale and circulation. Alexandria has a population of 150,000; say Moslems, 110,000; Greeks, 6,000; Jews, 4,000; Europeans and other foreigners, 30,000.

"I also visited the ruins of the Alexandrine Library, where our Septuagint translation of the Old Testament was made by order of Ptolemy Philadelphus, two hundred and eighty-four years before Christ, and the spot where it is said St. Mark the Evangelist suffered martyrdom, now occupied by a Turkish mosque of a thousand and one columns.

"Learning from the American Consul that a steamer would sail on the following day from Cairo for the upper Nile, accomplishing the voyage in seventeen days, which requires sixty in a Nile boat, I decided to improve this favorable opportunity for exploring Upper Egypt, as a field for circulating the Scriptures, and also to investigate the confirmations of Scripture history and prophecy, found upon the sculptured monuments and tombs of this ancient land. I accordingly provided myself with a small supply of Coptic and Arabic Bibles and Testaments, and took the morning train from Alexandria for Cairo, where we arrived the same afternoon, and embarked immediately on board the steamer for Assouan.

"I had been much interested in the Copts, the descendants of the ancient Egyptians, who never embraced the Mohammedan religion, though threatened with death, and suffering great persecutions from the Moslems; and thought they might afford an encouraging field for Bible distribution. They trace their descent to Copt, one of the four sons of Mizraim, the son of Ham, who settled in Egypt, and gained possession of the whole country. Egypt is styled, in Arabic, Misi, which recalls the old Hebrew Mizraim (Mizrim); in the ancient Egyptian language it was called Khemi, or, the land of Khem, answering to the land of Ham, or rather Khem, mentioned in the Bible.

"My first effort to introduce the Scriptures among them was at Girgeh, two days' sail from Cairo. As I was walking in the street I met two of them, distinguished by wearing the dark turban. I inquired for the church, and they at once conducted me there. It is neatly built of brick, has a matting covering the floor, and a gallery for the women above. I inquired also for their balas, or priest, and they soon brought him and several other chief men to see me. They asked me if I were Catholic. I said 'No.' 'Taib' (good), they exclaimed. I told them I was a Christian. 'Taib keteer' (good many times). I asked them if they wished the Scriptures. 'Eriva' (yes). I told them I had some at the steamer. They volunteered to come down in a body, fifteen or twenty, to receive them, and expressed the greatest delight when they opened the books, and read the Psalms and Gospel in their own Coptic language. I gave them six copies—all I could spare from my little stock, and still they urged for more. Two Mussulmans, who had followed us to the church and steamer, now came forward and commended the Christians, saying, 'Gepti taib keteer' (Copts are very good). It was pleasant to receive this testimony from Mohammedans, and to find such a spirit of harmony existing between them, instead of a feeling of hatred and persecution. I asked if all the Copts could read, and they took me to their school, near the church, where thirty or forty boys were diligently reading and studying from their plates or squares of tin, written with ink, which they use instead of printed books. I was informed that they number 2,500 in the town, and are the best educated and most intelligent portion of the people. In fact, they are the money-changers and secretaries of the Turkish officials, and without them the business of government could never be conducted.

"My next visit to them was at Esne, in Upper Egypt, where our steamer called for the passengers to view the ruins of an old temple. I was guided by one of them, whom I met in the street, to their principal church. They sent directly for the balas (priest) and several of the chief Copts. I asked if they had the Scriptures. They produced a copy of their liturgy in Coptic and Arabic, and expressed a great desire to have also 'Tourat and Ingil' (the Bible and Gospel). I tell them that I have some at the steamer if they wish. They answer, 'Taib,' and say they will come immediately to the river for them. They invite me first, however, into a large house near by, where several of their elders are seated. I join their circle after the Oriental manner, and tell them that 'I am American Inglese, that we love the Bible and the Copts, and I have come to give them this Book of God.' 'Taib keteer,' they exclaimed, 'Americani, gepti Christiani, sawa, sawa, sawa' (the Americans and Copts are Christian brothers), said they, putting the forefingers of their two hands together to express close friendship. I could speak but few words of Arabic, and one or two of them could speak only a few words in Turkish, so that we were obliged principally to employ the language of signs. As I spoke still to them of the Bible and Gospel, one of their number remarked, 'Allah var' (God is here). They then brought me coffee for refreshment, and the whole party came with me to receive the Scriptures. They formed quite a little procession of venerable men, headed by their old priest, Abraham, and his young assistant, John, and followed by a number of their children, I gave them a Bible and two Testaments. They expressed much gratitude, and said they would both read it, hide it in their hearts, and teach it also to their children. The priests, unlike the Catholics, were very desirous to have their people receive the Bible, and thanked me cordially for it in their name. An intelligent little boy, ten or twelve years of age, now came forward, and entreated me for an 'Ingil' (Testament). I asked if he could read it. A Testament was handed him, and he read it as fluently as a grown person. He kissed my hand, and begged me for a book by holding out his two hands before me; but I had no more to spare, and was obliged to refuse him. I thought, however, a 'backshish' would satisfy him as well, and placed a small piece of money in his hand. He at once gave it back to me with a smile, and put out his hands again entreating me for a book. I much regretted that I must deny him and others begging for 'Ingil Tourat,' and could only promise that I would send them more from Cairo by the first opportunity.

"Their priests are allowed to marry, and the Copts have one wife, and live together in families as Christians. They do not worship images, pictures, or saints, or pray to the Virgin Mary, as the Greeks and Catholics, but only to God through Christ alone. They have four churches, and number 1,500 in Esne. More than one-third, or 500, are able to read. At Assouan, the ancient Syene, I found the acting American Consul was a Copt, and twenty or thirty others resided in the village. They have no church or priest among them, but have a service every Sunday, and an address or sermon from one of their number. They desired much to have the Scriptures, and I gave them two copies of the New Testament, for which they brought me presents of ebony wood to express their gratitude in return. I requested the Consul to assemble them all at his house in the evening, and in company with several English and American friends made them a visit, and told them of our faith and worship in England and America. They heartily assented to all, and were delighted to receive instructions from us as Christians from distant lands. They had never before received any visit from missionaries or Christian friends, and it was indeed encouraging to preach the Gospel to these simple-minded Christian people, and give them the New Testament, far on the borders of Ethiopia. May the Lord bless his Word, that the desert may in truth bud and blossom as the rose, and Ethiopia stretch forth her hands unto God.

"On our return I learned that at ancient Thebes there is a large community of Copts, and a bishop living among them. The American Consul, though a Mussulman, said that his family and the bishop's were like brothers, and he would immediately send for him to meet me at his house. The bishop very soon came, and I was much pleased with his venerable, patriarchal appearance. I spoke to him of the Bible and Gospel, and related to him what I had already done for the Copts. He thanked me sincerely, and said, 'It is very kind in the Americans to remember the Copts; and I am exceedingly glad to have my people receive the Scriptures.' I then made an appointment to visit his church with him on the following day. The next morning I called upon him at his house. He gave me the Christian salutation and a welcome to his home. After the ordinary Oriental entertainment, we visited the two schools for boys which the bishop has instructed in his house, and then set out for the church. Having crossed the Nile, we rode on horseback for an hour across the sandy plain, quite to the base of the Lybian mountains, and came to the ancient Coptic church that stands alone on the edge of the desert. Here they were driven by Moslem persecution, and here they now toil up every Sabbath to worship God. It is a plain and simple edifice, built of plaster, and supported by old Corinthian columns from the ruins of a Christian church of the age of Constantine. As we sat upon the matting, resting from the heat of the sun, I asked the bishop what was the belief of his church respecting the Bible and Saviour. He answered, 'We believe that the Bible is from God: Christ is the Son of God. Glory be to the Father, Son, and Holy Ghost. Amen." I said to him that we would be glad to have him come to America, and tell us all about his people. He smiled and replied: "Yes, the Copts are very poor, and I would like much to visit America, and get money to build another church in the village, as it is so far to come across the sandy plain under a burning sun." We then returned, and at his house I found a number of the principal Copts assembled to meet me. I presented them with a copy of the Bible, and told them that we loved this Bible in America, and I had come to give it to those who have it not in the East. They gathered around me, and exclaimed, 'Mashallah' (God be praised). I asked the bishop if he wished to have American missionaries come and live among his people, to instruct them in the Scriptures and preach the Gospel, as they had done among the Armenians. He replied, 'I would be very happy to welcome American Christians among my people.' He then gave me his parting salutation, as they all did, in the name of God; and I returned on board our steamer for Cairo. I have thus been much interested in exploring the Coptic field, and distributing the Scriptures among this ancient Christian people."

At Constantinople Mr. Righter had become interested in the objects of the Evangelical Alliance, of which he was made the Corresponding Secretary, and he was charged with a special commission to advance the objects of the Alliance, by organizing similar associations in other places. He makes frequent mention in his notes of travel of organizing committees among those who loved the cause of Christ, after having explained to them the purposes aimed at in the Alliance.

CHAPTER XV.

VISIT TO PALESTINE.

Mr. Righter's stay in Egypt was short. The principal part of his time was spent in Cairo and the vicinity, and having accomplished all that seemed immediately practicable he returned to Alexandria, and took passage for Jaffa in company with Mr. and Mrs. Wm. C. Prime, whom he met in Egypt, Mr. De Leon, United States Consul to Egypt, and several other friends whom he had met since leaving Constantinople. It was quite a remarkable coincidence that he should be the travelling companion of three brothers in three separate years. When he left home for the first time in 1853, it was in company with Rev. S. Irenæus Prime, who was leaving to spend a year in foreign travel to restore his wasted health. Mr. R. was with him during that whole year of travel. When he set out a second time in 1854, it was in company with Rev. E. D. G. Prime, who was leaving to take charge of the American chapel at Rome, where they parted after being together nearly two months.

On reaching Egypt, in January, 1856, he very unexpectedly met with Mr. William C. Prime, with whom he afterwards travelled through the Holy Land and to Constantinople.

Arrived at Jaffa, Mr. R. says:—"I made a visit to the so-called house of one Simon, a tanner, by the sea side, where Simon Peter lodged, and as he went up on the housetop to pray, saw heaven opened, and a vision of four-footed beasts of the earth, and wild beasts, and creeping things, and fowls of the air, as it had been a great sheet knit at the four corners, and let down to the earth, teaching him that what God had cleansed, he should not call common or unclean; but that 'on the Gentiles also would be poured out the gift of the Holy Ghost,' and henceforth he became a preacher of righteousness to the Gentiles as well as the Jews.

"Thence I proceeded directly to Jerusalem, passing across the plain of Sharon and over the mountains of Judea. It was with peculiar emotions that we entered the Holy City, around which cluster so many hallowed associations, whence we received both the law and the Gospel; where our divine Saviour lived, taught, and died, rose from the dead, and ascended to the right hand of the Father, where 'he ever liveth to make intercession for us.' From the New World we have come to bring back the same Bible and Gospel in its purity to this distant land, whence we had received it through the apostles and primitive Christians 1,800 years ago."

He records his impressions more at length in his letters from which large extracts are made. The following letters were addressed to the editors of the "New York Observer:"

"At length 'our feet stand within thy gates, O Jerusalem.' 'Beautiful for situation, the joy of the whole earth is Mount Zion. Pray for the peace of Jerusalem: they shall prosper that love thee.' How rich and thrilling are the associations that throng upon the mind as you enter the Holy City. The abode of the prophets, apostles, and Saviour himself; where the sublime scenes of our faith transpired, atonement, resurrection, ascension; where the Holy Spirit descended on the day of Pentecost, to the disciples, in cloven tongues as of fire, and all spake in strange languages the wonderful works of God. Next to walking the golden streets of the new Jerusalem, to stand within the earthly city, and gain a vivid, realizing sense of these spiritual scenes, yields perhaps the highest joy to the Christian heart. To look upon Mount Zion, Mount Moriah, and the mountains round about Jerusalem, Gethsemane, Calvary, the Sepulchre, and the Mount of Ascension, where the heavens were opened, and the Saviour received into glory, quicken one's faith and zeal in the service of his Divine Master, as no other influence can, save the movings of the Spirit of God upon the heart.

"The first day that I spent in Jerusalem was one of the most deeply interesting of my life. In the morning (though not the Sabbath), we attended service in the English church upon Mount Zion, an elegant Gothic building, and a fitting sanctuary to worship God in his ancient chosen dwelling-place. The Scriptures were read, embracing the preaching of John the Baptist, 'Prepare ye the way of the Lord, make his paths straight. Every valley shall be filled, and every mountain and hill shall be brought low; and the crooked shall be made straight, and the rough ways shall be made smooth: and all flesh shall see the salvation of God.' Also the baptism of Jesus, when 'the heaven was opened, and the Holy Ghost descended in a bodily shape like a dove upon him, and a voice came from heaven, which said, Thou art my beloved Son: in thee I am well pleased.' The Gospel comes to us as the oracles of salvation from the lips of the earnest preacher, and the songs of praise, and the voice of prayer ascend as incense before the throne, to call down the blessing of heaven upon the worshipping assembly. Surely, 'this is none other than the house of God, this is the gate of heaven,' to our souls, and here we do sit together in heavenly places in Christ Jesus.

"It was a scene and impression never to be forgotten. 'They that trust in the Lord shall be as Mount Zion, which cannot be removed, but abideth for ever.' 'As the mountains are round about Jerusalem, so the Lord is round about his people, from henceforth, even for ever.' After service, we were introduced to good Bishop Gobat, and an excellent circle of Christian friends, faithful watchmen on the walls of Zion. Then we went forth in company with Dr. Bonar, of Scotland, and Dr. Tyler, of America, to gain our first views and impressions of the holy city, and the sacred localities around.

"We first examined the town of David, a quadrangular fortress built in the walls upon the western side of Mount Zion. It is partly of modern, and partly of ancient construction. The lower stones are large, and leveled in the ancient Jewish style of workmanship, which is as distinctly marked as the Roman or Grecian. The foundation must therefore undoubtedly be referred to the time of David when he took the fortress of Mount Zion from the Jebusites, and strengthened it, and made Jerusalem the capital of his kingdom. Then passing beyond the Jaffa gate, and ascending a flight of stone steps, we climbed to the top of the city walls. They are built of square masses of limestone, and strengthened with towers and battlements in the Saracenic style. A wide space is left upon the top, and a parapet upon the outer edge gives security to the walk that commands a beautiful view both within and without the city. From this point at the northwest angle of Mount Zion, we looked westward to the upper and lower pools and valley of Gihon, that terminates in the valley of the Sons of Hinnom. It is recorded that 'Hezekiah stopped the upper water course of Gihon, and brought it straight down to the west side of the city of David.' This aqueduct is still traceable, and conducts underneath the walls to the pool of Hezekiah within the city. At this fountain of Gihon, Zadok the priest took an horn of oil out of the Tabernacle and anointed Solomon king of Israel. 'And they blew the trumpet, and all the people said, God save king Solomon. And all the people came up after him, and the people piped with pipes, and rejoiced with great joy, so that the earth rent with the sound of them.'

"As we looked down upon this valley, and the reservoir still remaining, around which the anointing of the Wise King was celebrated, the whole scene was vividly impressed upon the mind. From this point also we traced the course and direction of the ancient walls of the city, and the whole was spread out as a physical map before us. Turning to the right we saw the gardens of Bathsheba within the walls now planted with green growing grain, and portions of Mount Zion under the plough of cultivation. 'Zion shall be ploughed like a field.' Also piles of ruin and rubbish were heaped around, and an air of desolation prevailed, like a city overthrown. 'Jerusalem shall become heaps, behold your house is left unto you desolate.' The whole not only forcibly illustrated Scripture history, but also the terrible fulfilment of Scripture prophecy pronounced against the covenant people for their transgression and unbelief. We now continue our walk upon the walls, and come to the Damascus gate on the North, that forms the great public way to Samaria and Galilee. Before us on the left is Mount Scopus, where Titus pitched his camp and displayed his army to the Jews before attacking the city, thinking they would at once surrender at the sight of the Roman legions, but they were doomed to a more fearful destruction, that the Saviour's prophecy might be literally fulfilled. 'And they shall fall by the edge of the sword, and shall be led away captive into all nations; and Jerusalem shall be trodden down of the Gentiles until the times of the Gentiles be fulfilled.' 'And as some spake of the temple, how it was adorned with goodly stones and gifts,' he said, 'As for these things which ye behold, the days will come in the which there shall not be left one stone upon another, that shall not be thrown down.' Titus was most anxious to save the temple, as one of the noblest monuments of ancient art. But the 'holy and beautiful house,' says the Jewish historian, 'was destined to destruction,' and through a 'divine impulse,' a Roman soldier seized a burning brand and cast it in at the golden window, whereby the whole edifice was soon wrapt in flames. Titus hastened to the spot, and finding all attempt to save the building hopeless, entered the sanctuary and directed the removal of the sacred utensils of gold, some of which afterwards graced his triumphal procession, and were sculptured upon the arch that commemorated his victory at Rome, where they may be seen to this day.

"Continuing our walk, we reached the northeast angle of the wall. The valley of Jehosaphat is below, and the course through which the brook Kedron winds its way. There, too, is the garden of Gethsemane, enclosed within a wall, and containing six ancient olive trees (supposed by many to be the same that were standing in the time of our Saviour), where he fell upon his face and prayed, saying, 'O my Father, if it be possible let this cup pass from me; nevertheless, not as I will but as thou wilt.' Here, or at least not far off, the Saviour endured that 'agony and bloody sweat,' which betokened that the redemption of a sinful world rested upon his soul, and well nigh crushed the human nature with its weight. 'And there appeared an angel unto him from heaven strengthening him.' Beyond rises the beautiful Mount of Olives, the favorite place of retirement to our Saviour and his disciples, from the noise and distraction of the city for divine meditation and prayer. 'And in the day time he was teaching in the temple, and at night he went out and abode in the mount that is called the Mount of Olives.' Here, also, upon this hillside, just without the walls of the city, was doubtless the scene of the crucifixion. It was outside the city in a public place, for 'they that passed by reviled on him, wagging their heads,' and saying, 'Thou that destroyest the temple and buildest it in three days, save thyself. If thou be the Son of God, come down from the cross.'

"The high road to Huathoth runs near this place. And just across this little valley, on the slope of Olivet, the women may have stood and beheld afar off. 'And many women were there, (beholding afar off,) which followed Jesus from Galilee, ministering unto him.'

"The sepulchre, too, was probably here. This was a place of gardens and private tombs of wealthy Jews. The hillside is still filled with sepulchres and tombs, cut in the solid rock. 'Now in the place where he was crucified there was a garden; and in the garden a new sepulchre, wherein was never man yet laid. There laid they Jesus, therefore, because of the Jews' preparation day! for the sepulchre was nigh at hand.'

"Here, then, our Saviour suffered on the cross and made atonement for the sins of the world. Here he was laid in the grave, and burst the bonds of death, that all through faith might walk in the newness of life. Here, then, our hopes of salvation and immortal life centre and cling, waiting for the manifestation of the sons of God, knowing that when Christ appeareth we shall be like him, for we shall see him as he is.

"How greatly was our faith strengthened and zeal quickened by looking upon these scenes.

"We continued our walk upon the city walls, and came to St. Stephen's gate, and the wall of the harem, that surrounds the court of the mosque of Omar. Beyond this, Moslem bigotry will allow no Christian foot to tread, without special orders from their Pasha. Descending thence we passed through the gate, and beside the rock where the first of martyrs for the Gospel suffered death. 'He, being full of the Holy Ghost, looked up steadfastly into heaven, and saw the glory of

God and Jesus standing on the right hand of God. And they stoned Stephen, calling upon God, and saying, Lord Jesus, receive my spirit.' What a halo of glory surrounds the death of this devoted preacher of righteousness so soon after the crucifixion and resurrection of Christ; whose earnest zeal in the service of his Master caused his face to shine as it had been the face of an angel; and whose triumphant faith saw the heavens opened and the Son of Man standing on the right hand of God. Pursuing the path across the valley and bed of the brook Kedron, we walked up the old footpath toward Bethany. Here are ancient steps cut in the rock over which our Saviour often walked to visit Mary, and her sister Martha, and Lazarus whom he loved. Just at the right are the large stones on which it is said the disciples slept, when Jesus withdrew for prayer in Gethsemane, saying unto them, 'My soul is exceeding sorrowful, even unto death: tarry ye here and watch with me.' 'And he cometh unto the disciples and findeth them asleep. And he went away again the second time and prayed, and he came and found them asleep. The third time also he cometh to his disciples and saith unto them: Sleep on now and take your rest; behold he is at hand that doth betray me.' A granite column marks the spot, it is said, where Judas betrayed his Master with a kiss, and delivered him to the multitude with swords and staves, who came from the chief priests and elders of the people, to take Jesus, that they might put him to death.

"Passing on and ascending the side of the Mount of Olives, we reached the place where our Saviour beheld the city, wept over it, and predicted its ruin, saying: 'For the days shall come upon thee that thine enemies shall cast a trench about thee, and compass thee round, and keep thee in on every side, and shall lay thee even with the ground, and thy children within thee; and they shall not leave in thee one stone upon another, because thou knewest not the time of thy visitation.' How literally was this accomplished by the Romans under Titus. The historian tells us 'the folly of resistance was so clear to Titus, that he became exasperated at the unpleasant task which their obstinacy imposed upon him. He raised around the city a *strong wall of circumvallation, strengthened with towers*, resolved that none of them should escape but such as surrendered to him.' Thus Titus became the unconscious instrument of accomplishing that doom of the city which Christ had nearly forty years before denounced. The whole city lay extended like a map before us. We could see and distinguish the streets, and the whole interior to the inner ride of the farther wall. First and most conspicuous are seen the walls of the harem, the court and the mosque of Omar, upon the broad summit of Mount Moriah, the site of Solomon's temple. The grounds are covered with greensward, and planted with olive and cypress trees, that form a picturesque feature in the view. Beyond stands Mount Zion, crowned with the American convent and the English Protestant church, and on the right are the domes of the church of Calvary and the Holy Sepulchre; while the Moslem minarets, rising at intervals between, tell us that the followers of the false prophet still bear sway in the holy city. It was indeed a lovely view, when we remember the divine glory manifested and the wondrous scenes that have transpired here.

"We then ascended still higher the side of Mount Olivet, and visited the cave or tombs of the prophets. They consist of chambers and passages that extend far in the mountain. In some places they are very narrow and explored with much difficulty. Returning thence, we walked through the Jewish burial ground upon the side of the mountain looking toward Jerusalem. The Jews love to be buried here, because they say their Messiah will come and stand upon the Mount of Olives, and they will then rise to dwell and reign with him in the restored city and kingdom of Israel. Then we came to Absalom's Pillar in the valley of Jehoshaphat. It is cut in the solid rock of the mountain, to which the base is still attached, and is in the form of a circular pyramid upon a pedestal ornamented with sixteen Ionic columns. A large hole has been broken at the side, and Jewish children are taught to throw stones into it, in contempt for the unnatural rebellion of Absalom against his father David. There is very little evidence, however, that this is the identical pillar that 'Absalom reared up for himself in the king's dale,' because he said, 'I have no son to keep my name in remembrance.' In the rear of this monument is the tomb of Jehoshaphat, said to be filled with ancient manuscripts of the law. And just below is the tomb or grotto of St. James, extending into the side of the Mount of Olives. Here, it is said, the apostle took refuge in a time of persecution and distress. Just below stands the so-called tomb of Zechariah, who was 'slain between the temple and the altar.' It is also of pyramidal form and hewn out of the solid rock. Each of its sides is ornamented with six Ionic columns, and a broad cornice runs around the shaft. No visible entrance to the interior has yet been discovered.

"It is doubtful whether any of these monuments can be truly assigned to the persons whose names they bear. They appear to be of the Egyptian style of architecture intermingled with Grecian ornaments.

"We now crossed the valley and ascended again to the walls of the city. Passing underneath the golden gateway, now closed, we observed the beautiful columns of verd antique and marble thrust into the wall by the Turks, and examined the immense blocks of stone on which the foundation rests, some of which measured twenty-four feet in length by four in thickness, and are doubtless a portion of the outer wall of Solomon's temple remaining in position to this day. They are dressed and beveled in the peculiar Jewish style of workmanship, and no cement is used in joining them together.

"Turning the southeast angle of the wall, we discovered an inverted tablet inserted near the top, containing a Latin inscription partly effaced, to Hadriano Diro Augusto, etc., probably a slab from the temple of Jupiter, which that Emperor erected on the site of the Jewish temple. Ascending the south side of Mount Zion, we looked down the valley of the Tyropoeon to the pool of Siloam, and the king's gardens that are watered from this fountain. Beyond is the well of Nehemiah and En-rogel, where Jonathan and Ahimaaz waited to bring intelligence to David when he was driven from the city by the rebellion of Absalom. Higher up in the valley of the Son of

Hinnom is Tophet, where the children of Judah built the high places to burn their sons and their daughters in the fire, for which sin the Lord brought signal judgments upon his chosen people.

"The sun had just set behind the mountains of Judea, and the moon rose beautifully over the Mount of Olives, as we entered Zion gate and returned to our home within the city.

"We have thus 'walked about Zion and gone round about her: told the towers thereof, marked well her bulwarks, and considered her palaces;' and rejoice to say with the Psalmist, 'This God is our God for ever and ever; he will be our guide even unto death.'

"In the evening we ascended to our house-top on Mount Zion, and enjoyed a moonlight view of the city,—the Mount of Olives and the mountains of Moab in the distance. The sky of the Orient was pure and bright, the moon and stars were shining with celestial beauty, and in the presence of the scene we could not but call to mind the exclamation of the Psalmist: 'When I consider the heavens, the work of thy fingers: the moon and stars, which thou hast ordained: what is man that thou art mindful of him? and the son of man that thou visitest him?'

"We rose early this morning to enjoy the sunrise view from our house-top on Mount Zion. The morning star was in the east, and the dawn lovely with purple and rosy light. Then came the reddening rays as the sun shone glorious over Moab, lighting up Olivet, the minarets of the city, the domes of Omar and the Holy Sepulchre, flooding the streets with golden light, falling upon Gihon and the mountains of Judea beyond, and filling the entire landscape with new life and beauty. The moon was just sinking in the west as the sun was rising in the east, and the whole formed a scene of transcendant beauty, such as I have never before witnessed in the Orient. In the language of the Psalmist, 'The heavens declare the glory of God, and the firmament showeth his handiwork. In them hath he set a tabernacle for the sun, *which is as a bridegroom coming out of his chamber, and rejoiceth as a strong man to run a race.*' We then went to visit the tomb of David upon the southern summit of Mount Zion, without the walls. It was formerly a Christian church, now converted into a Mohammedan mosque, and is regarded by Moslems, Jews, and Christians as enclosing the sepulchre of Israel's king. With some difficulty, we succeeded in gaining admittance to the room where the tomb stands. It is built in the Mohammedan style, covered over with a green cloth, and filled upon the outer surface with the names of Jews in Hebrew characters, who have been privileged to visit the place. It is greatly venerated by the Jews, as occupying the precise spot where the royal dust of David reposes; and they frequently resort to the next chamber, near as Moslem bigotry will permit them, to weep over their fallen condition.

"In an adjoining part of the building we were shown the large 'upper room,' where it is said the Saviour celebrated the last passover with his disciples. They also point to a recess in the wall as the seat occupied by Jesus on that occasion. The room is now used for religious services by the native Christians, and the Moslems also have a praying place here, looking towards Mecca. It is remarkable that Mohammedans hold many of the localities connected with the patriarchs and prophets of Old Testament history in even greater veneration than the Christians and Jews. But they seldom reverence any that pertain to the life, death, and resurrection of Christ, though they regard Jesus as the last and greatest of prophets before Mahomet. Upon leaving the mosque, we passed a ruined stone wall, where it is said the Virgin Mary lived with the beloved disciple, John, in his own house after the crucifixion. It is greatly venerated by the Latin, Greek, and Armenian pilgrims, and several were here, crossing, prostrating themselves, and kissing the stones of the wall.

"Then we visited the American convent near by which they tell us occupies the site of the house of Caiaphas, the high-priest, where they led away Jesus the night after his arrest in the garden of Gethsemane. The place of the Saviour's imprisonment and mocking is here shown, also where the Apostle Peter denied his Lord, when the cock crew, and Peter went out and wept bitterly. Likewise behind the altar, they have a large, rough block of stone, which is said to be the identical stone that was rolled before the door of the Saviour's sepulchre. The pilgrims kiss it with much devotion, and bedew its surface with many tears. Though Protestant travellers, overcome by the emotions of the place and hour, frequently yield implicit belief in all these sacred relics and localities, I am rather inclined to conclude, that for wise reasons, for the most part, they are entirely lost. Yet one cannot but have his faith strengthened, and devotion quickened, by visiting the precise spots where tradition relates that these scenes of the Saviour's mission upon earth were witnessed.

"Entering Zion gate, we now pass the lepers' quarter, a few miserable hovels near the city walls. They live apart by themselves, are outcasts from society, and are obliged always to intermarry with each other. Consequently, not only themselves but their children are all afflicted with this loathsome disease. No sympathy seems extended to them, and they are suffered to live and die in filth and wretchedness, the most pitiable objects in the world.

"Continuing our walk, we came to the outer walls of the haram or court of the mosque of Omar. Here we examined the immense stones forming the arch discovered by Dr. Robinson, that spanned the valley between Mount Moriah and Mount Zion. They bear marks of great antiquity, and were doubtless connected with the works of Solomon's temple.

"Then passing through the filthy Jewish quarter, we visited the wailing-place of the Jews opposite the large stones of the old temple wall. Here fifteen or sixteen old men and as many women and children, were standing opposite the wall reading the Hebrew prophecies, weeping and wailing over the desolation of Jerusalem, and praying that their long-expected Messiah would come and build again the wastes of Zion. They bowed down with their faces to a hole in the corner of the wall, and as they turned away their eyes were wet with tears, and their faces filled with sorrow and grief. It was indeed an affecting scene, yet I was more than ever impressed with the stubborn unbelief of the Jews, who still reject the Saviour before the very ruins of the temple whose destruction he predicted eighteen hundred years ago.

"Returning thence near St. Stephen's gate, we

met with an old Franciscan monk, who walked with us along the 'via dolorosa,' and pointed out the various traditional localities connected with the trial and death of Christ. 'Here,' said he, 'stood the palace of Pontius Pilate the Roman governor, where the chief-priests and elders of the people led away Jesus bound from the house Caiaphas, and delivered him up to be falsely accused and condemned to death. And when Pilate found no cause of death in him, but would release him and let him go, the multitude cried out, His blood be on us and on our children; crucify him! crucify him!' Just upon our right is the chapel of flagellation, where the soldiers scourged Jesus, arrayed him in scarlet robes, platted a crown of thorns and put it upon his head, spit upon him, and mocked, saying, 'Hail, King of the Jews!' An old arch standing across the street is called *Ecce Homo*, where Pilate said unto them, as Jesus came forth wearing the crown of thorns and the purple robe, Behold the man! Then he delivered him unto them to be crucified. And they took Jesus and led him away, and he went forth bearing his cross. As we walked along this mournful way, 'Here,' said the monk, 'our Saviour cried Salva Mater, and there by that granite column they laid hold upon Simon of Cyrene to bear his cross. This upon our right was the house of Lazarus, and that yonder the palace of the rich man of whom our Saviour spake in parables.' We then ascended the hill to the churches of Calvary and the Holy Sepulchre, both included under the same roof. It is a large and imposing edifice, entered from an open court fronted by two broad towers in the semi-gothic style. The centre is crowned by the dome of the Holy Sepulchre, and upon the right rises the smaller dome of Calvary. We first ascended a flight of twenty-two stone steps to the top of Mount Calvary. The floor is laid with marble, and just in front of an altar dedicated to the Virgin, a hole is cut, through which you see where the cross stood, and also a deep rent in the rock underneath made by the earthquake at the crucifixion.

"Descending thence by a long passage and another flight of thirty-one steps, we visited a dark chapel dedicated to St. Helena, where, it is said, the three crosses were found, that of our Saviour and the two thieves who were crucified with him. Upon our return a marble slab is shown to us as the stone on which the body of the Saviour was anointed previous to burial. Then we enter the sepulchre itself under a marble canopy richly decorated with lamps of silver and gold, kept burning night and day. In a small inner chamber stands a marble sarcophagus in which, it is said, our Saviour was laid, and from which he rose from the dead. Two black-veiled nuns entered just before me, and kissed and bedewed the marble with their tears. It is profoundly reverenced by the Latin and Oriental Christians, though it bears no evidence of being the true sepulchre. In front also stands a small marble block, on which they say the angel sat who announced to the women first visiting the sepulchre the resurrection of our Lord. Upon the right as we came out, the Greeks have a marble pillar fixed in the pavement, surrounded by a railing, which they say occupies the centre of the earth, and marks the precise spot whence the earth was taken, of which Adam was created. In a side-chapel upon the left, the Latins also point out the stone column to which our Saviour was bound, and the block whereon the Roman soldiers cast lots for his vesture. Just behind the sepulchre are likewise shown the tombs of Adam and Joseph of Arimathea, hewn in the natural rock. It is now the time of Easter pilgrimage, and multitudes of devout worshippers are crossing and prostrating themselves before these sacred localities. Such are the absurd and idolatrous superstitions that are believed and perpetuated year after year (through their bishops and priests) by the thousands of pilgrims who visit the churches of Calvary and the Holy Sepulchre.

"C. N. R."

CHAPTER XVI.

BETHANY AND BETHLEHEM.

"As we had now visited the principal places of interest within and around Jerusalem, we proposed this morning a visit to the village of Bethany. Walking out at the Damascus gate on the North, and continuing along the city walls, we came to the grotto of Jeremiah, an ancient cave or quarry, hewn in the limestone rock. There is now a neat little garden enclosed by a wall in front, and a Mohammedan dervish has built a mosque and praying place within it. We refreshed ourselves at the well and then continued on our way past St. Stephen's gate, and by a winding path to the valley of Jehoshaphat and the brook Kedron, and at length came upon the high road to Jericho. This is the same road our Saviour was often wont to walk on his visits to Bethany. But how changed the scene. Then the ancient covenant people filled the Holy City, and the splendid temple of Herod crowned the height of Mount Moriah. Now the Moslem mosque of Omar rises there, and we hear the

Muezzin cry to prayer as we ascend along the side of Olivet. Jerusalem is trodden down of the Gentiles, even of the followers of the false prophet, who curse alike the name of Jew and Christian. Yet she shall rise again. Thus saith the Lord, 'Rejoice ye with Jerusalem; I will extend peace to her like a river, and the glory of the Gentiles like a flowing stream: for the law shall go forth of Zion, and the word of the Lord from Jerusalem.'

"In a half hour more we came to Bethany, the town of Mary and her sister Martha, with whom Jesus loved to dwell. It is beautifully situated in a quiet little valley at the base of the Mount of Olives, and seems a fitting place for our Saviour's retirement and social enjoyment. With this one family more than any other on earth, he held personal communion and fellowship, and his affectionate tenderness flowed forth to them in all its blessed fulness. Here it was that Mary anointed the feet of Jesus with precious ointment, very costly, and wiped his feet with her hair, to testify her love for the Saviour. And when she was rudely rebuked by Judas Iscariot, Jesus replied, 'Let her alone; why trouble ye her? She hath wrought a good work on me. Verily I say unto you, wheresoever this gospel shall be preached throughout the whole world, this also that she hath done shall be spoken of for a memorial of her.' Here also Jesus raised Lazarus from the dead. We at once sought out the grave of Lazarus, and were pointed to a large tomb excavated in the natural rock and bearing many marks of antiquity. Descending a flight of twenty-seven stone steps, we came to a dark room eight or nine feet square, which conducted to a second arched chamber. This was doubtless the place where the body was laid and the stone placed upon the door of the sepulchre. 'It was a cave and a stone lay upon it,' says the Evangelist John. Here, then, at the entrance of this very cave, in all probability, Jesus wrought the great miracle of raising Lazarus from the dead. How sublime was the scene. Jesus said, 'Take ye away the stone.' Then they took away the stone from the place where the dead was laid. And Jesus lifted up his eyes and said, 'Father, I thank thee that thou hast heard me; and I knew that thou hearest me always; but because of the people which stand by I said it, that they may believe that thou hast sent me. And when he had thus spoken, he cried with a loud voice, Lazarus come forth. And he that was dead came forth, bound hand and foot with grave clothes, and his face was bound about with a napkin. Jesus saith unto them, Loose him and let him go.' I was nowhere so impressed with a sense of the divinity of Christ as when standing beside the grave of Lazarus.

He spake and the departed spirit heard his voice, and returned to bring the dead body from the tomb, and restore the brother to his loving sisters. Surely this was not the work of man, but of God, even the God-Man, Christ Jesus. He wept at the door of the sepulchre, to testify how tenderly he loved him. He prayed to his Father in heaven to signify that he came forth from the Father. He called the dead to life to manifest his dominion over the spirit world, that 'all might see the glory of God,' and believe that he was 'the resurrection aud the life, and that whosoever believeth in him shall never die.'

"We loved to linger long around this sepulchre and feel our faith strengthened that we, at last, through the same divine power, would triumph over death and the grave and rise to immortal life. The air was mild and lovely, the birds were singing sweetly, amid the blossoms of the almond trees, and all things were in harmony with the scene.

"On our return we took the foot-path across the side of Olivet, where Christ so often walked, and ascended to the summit of the Mount. Here tradition has falsely located the place of our Saviour's ascension. Whereas the Evangelist Luke expressly declares that 'he led them out as far as to *Bethany*. And he lifted up his hands and blessed them. And it came to pass while he blessed them, he was parted from them and carried up into heaven.' Now this point is perhaps only half the distance from Jerusalem to Bethany, and manifestly cannot be the place of the ascen sion, yet the oriental Christians have erected here a church and piously consecrated the spot. The Moslems have converted the church into a mosque, and guard it with zealous care. We are permitted to enter, however, and are pointed to a footprint of our Saviour on a rock under the centre, the last that he left on earth when he ascended to heaven. It is much worn by the kisses of pilgrims. Ascending the minaret, we enjoyed a splendid view of Mount Moriah, Mount Zion and the Holy City on the one side, and on the other the beautiful valley of the Jordan, the waters of the Dead Sea, the Mount of Temptation, and the mountains of Moab beyond, all forming a panorama of nature in the verdure and bloom of early spring.

"Such scenes as these, filled with all their sacred and hallowed associations, yield the highest joy to the Christian traveller. He seems in his journey to have reached the Delectable Mountains, whence he can well-nigh see the gates of the Celestial City.

"We passed the night in Bethlehem, the birthplace of the sweet singer of Israel and the Saviour of the world—what sacred associations gather to the scene, and what hallowed memories will ever cluster around it! In the morning early, I was awakened by the sound of singing, and hastened to attend high mass of the Armenians in the Grotto of the Nativity. It consisted of chanting by priests and small boys, bearing lighted candles, bowing, crossing, prostrations and kissing of the pavement by the pilgrims—similar ceremonies, though even more corrupt than the Catholic church; and as I stood by and witnessed this heartless worship, I could not but breathe forth the prayer that the time might speedily come when the gospel in its simplicity and purity will prevail in all the lands and languages of the Orient.

"What a cloud of darkness will roll away and a weight of ignorance and superstition be removed, when the day shall dawn and the day-star arise anew in the East.

"Returning thence, we were served with a comfortable breakfast by a Latin monk, and then set out upon our journey to Hebron. The country around Bethlehem is beautiful and well cultivated. The soil is fertile, and the hillsides and valleys are covered with olives, figs, pomegranates and terraced vineyards, which afford a picturesque view in the morning sunlight. In one hour we reached the pools of Solomon. They are situated upon a sloping hillside that forms the entrance of a valley winding eastward toward Jerusalem, and are immense in extent. They consist of three grand and deep basins walled with square stones and lined with cement, while the bottom is formed of the natural rock. The whole is so arranged that the stream from each flows into that below, and the lower pool is connected with a strongly built aqueduct that conducts to Jerusalem and the cisterns of Solomon's temple. A large fountain of four springs continually supplies them with pure and living water. It is indeed a splendid work considering the age in which it was constructed, and remains almost entire unto the present day.

"The pools were probably connected with pleasure grounds and a country palace of Solomon built upon this site. As he himself relates in Ecclesiastes: 'I made me great works; I builded me houses; I planted me vineyards; I made me gardens and orchards; I planted trees in them of all kinds of fruit. I made me *pools of water* to water therewith the wood that bringeth forth trees."

"Josephus also doubtless alludes to these pools in the following passage:—'There was a certain place about fifty furlongs distant from Jerusalem, which is called Etham. Very pleasant it is in fine gardens and abounding in rivulets of water. Thither did he (Solomon) use to go out in the morning, sitting on high in his chariot.' In their full and pristine beauty, surrounded by houses, vineyards, gardens, orchards and fruit trees, they must have been truly magnificent beyond description. Our path now winds over a rough rocky road, and barren, desolate country, though bearing evidence of former cultivation. We pass two ancient wells and tombs cut in the rocks by the wayside, and then come to a beautiful valley planted with vines carefully terraced upon the hillsides and filled with lodges and watchtowers to guard them in the season of vintage. This is the valley of Eshcol. And these luxuriant vineyards apparently still produce clusters of grapes equal to that which the spies 'cut down and bare between two upon a staff' unto Moses and Aaron, at Kadesh, in the wilderness of Paran, when they returned from searching out the land. Pomegranates, figs, and olives, also abound in this fertile valley at the present day.

"Just beyond, commanding a lovely view of the plain in front, is Hebron, called by the Arabs El-Khulil, 'the Friend,' marking it as the dwelling-place of Abraham, 'the Friend of God.' There is perhaps no city in Palestine so rich in ancient Scripture history as Hebron. Here the patriarchs, Abraham, Isaac, and Jacob, lived and walked with God: and here with their wives by their side, they all lie buried in the cave of the field of Machpelah, before Mamre; the same is Hebron in the land of Canaan. Here Abram when he separated from Lot 'removed his tent and came and dwelt in the plain of Mamre, which is in Hebron, and built there an altar unto the Lord.' 'And when Abram was ninety years old and nine, the Lord appeared to Abram, and said unto him, I am the Almighty God, walk before me and be thou perfect. And I will make my covenant between me and thee, and will multiply thee exceedingly. Neither shall thy name any more be called Abram; but thy name shall be Abraham; for a father of many nations have I made thee. And I will establish my covenant between me and thee, and thy seed after thee, in their generations, for an everlasting covenant; to be a God unto thee and thy seed after thee. And I will give unto thee, and to thy seed after thee, the land wherein thou art a stranger; all the land of Canaan, for an everlasting possession; and I will be their God.'

"And the Lord appeared again unto Abraham 'in the plains of Mamre, as he sat in the tent-door in the heat of the day,' and announced to him the birth of his son Isaac, in his old age, in whom all the nations of the earth should be blessed. Here also Abraham pleaded with the Lord to save the guilty cities of the plain from destruction, and not to slay the righteous with the wicked, until God promised that if peradventure ten righteous were found therein, he would not destroy it.

'And Abraham gat up early in the morning to the place where he stood before the Lord; and he looked toward Sodom and Gomorrah, and toward all the land of the plain, and beheld and lo! the smoke of the country went up as the smoke of a furnace.' In Hebron also Isaac long dwelt, and Jacob, after his years of service in Padan Aram, 'came unto Isaac his father, unto Mamre, unto the city of Arbah, which is Hebron, where Abraham and Isaac sojourned.' From hence he went down with his sons unto Pharaoh in Egypt, and became a great nation, and when Jacob was about 'to be gathered to his fathers' he commanded his sons saying, 'Bury me with my fathers, in the cave that is in the field of Machpelah, which is before Mamre in the land of Canaan; there they buried Abraham and Sarah his wife; there they buried Isaac and Rebekah his wife; and there I buried Leah. And his sons did unto him according as he commanded them. And Joseph went up to bury his father, and with him went up all the servants of Pharaoh, the elders of his house, and all the elders of the land of Egypt.' A grand funeral procession across the sands of the desert to bury the embalmed body of the aged patriarch in the land where his fathers dwelt and died and were buried.

"Hebron likewise became the capital of David's kingdom, where he reigned seven and a half years over Judah, and was also anointed king over all Israel. Here, too, he doubtless composed many of his sublime psalms, that have in all ages penetrated the soul and lifted it from earth to heaven. How vivid and thrilling were all these sacred associations, as just before the hour of sunset we passed through the vineyards of Eshcol, crossed the plain of Mamre, and came to the city of Hebron.

"We spent the night at the house of a Jew from Holland, who represented himself as the American consul of the place. The steps and floors were as neat as Dutch scrubbing and scouring could make them, but the fleas and other small animals were as abundant as the grapes in the valley of Eshcol in the most fruitful season. I found it convenient to go out upon the house-top at night and meditate, and the view in the clear starlight, of the plain, the valley, and the hills stretching far away, was beautiful indeed. There, too, I experienced a peculiar delight in holding communion and fellowship with the God of Abraham, Isaac, and Jacob, who had here often appeared to them and talked with them as friend talketh with his friend.

"In the morning we set out to visit the great mosque that is built over the cave of Machpelah, where the patriarchs are buried. This is regarded as one of the most undoubted localities of the

Holy Land, and is also esteemed one of the holiest places by the Mohammedans, who have the highest reverence for Abraham and the patriarchs; and on this account Christians are rigorously prevented from entering it. They were formerly not even allowed to approach near the outer walls of the harem. We were, however, unmolested in examining the exterior of the edifice. The structure is exceeding massive and has in all respects an ancient appearance. The walls are built of large stones levelled in the peculiar Jewish style, and similar to those around the court of the Mosque of Omar at Jerusalem. A number of square pillars, half imbedded in the wall, also extend around the building, and these are surmounted by a kind of cornice which gives to the whole an imposing effect.

"We then called upon the sheik of the mosque, Hadji Halil, to gain admittance, if possible, into the interior. He is a venerable, amiable-looking Mussulman, with a long, flowing white beard. He received us very kindly, and at once admitted us through the large gate within the outer wall. As we were about to ascend the broad steps that lead to the mosque, however, a crowd of bigoted Moslems gathered around and declared in the name of the prophet, that we should not be permitted to enter. The old sheik then conducts us in a very friendly manner to his own house within the court that overlooks the building and the grounds around, remarking at the same time, 'I myself would gladly admit you. There is nothing in my religion to forbid it, Mohammedans and Christians are all children of God and brothers together (most liberal sentiments to come from a Moslem sheik), but I dare not do it. My enemies would at once excite opposition and create an insurrection in the town.' Meanwhile he gives us a very hospitable entertainment of coffee, raisins, fruit, &c., in oriental style, and favors us with many interesting items of Mohammedan tradition in regard to the lives and history of the ancient patriarchs. It was most pleasant to find such a spirit of enlarged kindness and liberality in a Moslem dwelling in Hebron, where they are reputed the most bigoted and fanatical in all Palestine. Departing thence, we rode a short distance from the town to visit the large terebinth tree called 'Abraham's oak.' We found many acorns upon the ground, and also some upon the tree. It is of immense dimensions, very venerable and of great antiquity. Returning on our way, we soon came in sight of Nebby Jonas—'the grave of the Prophet Jonas.' Here the pilgrims have erected piles of stones, as is their custom, to mark their first point of view of a prophet's tomb. Then retracing rapidly our course, we at length come in sight of Mount Moriah and Jerusalem.

And we are reminded of the journey of Abraham over the same path, from Beersheba to the land of Moriah, at the command of the Lord, to offer up his only son Isaac upon one of the mountains there. 'Then on the third day Abraham lifted up his eyes and saw the place afar off.'

"As we approached, the sun was gilding the mountains of Moab, the summit of Olivet, the domes, minarets, and towers of the Holy City with purple and golden light, reminding us also of 'the New Jerusalem,' with its walls garnished with precious stones, its gates of pearl and streets of pure gold, 'wherein shall in nowise enter anything that defileth; neither whatsoever worketh abomination or maketh a lie; but they which are written in the Lamb's book of life, and the glory of God doth lighten it, and the Lamb is the light thereof.'

"How constant and lasting are such scenes to the Christian traveller in the Holy Land, and how they fondly linger in memory like a spiritual vision to elevate the soul from earth to heaven.

"C. N. R."

CHAPTER XVII.

JORDAN AND THE DEAD SEA.

"We made our next excursion from Jerusalem to the Jordan and the Dead Sea. Passing out of the Jaffa gate, and crossing the aqueduct from Solomon's pools, we rode along the valley of Hinnom, and passed Aceldama, or the Field of Blood, filled with caves, sepulchres, and dead men's bones. This was long used as a burial-place for strangers, and is at present entirely neglected and despised. The brook Kidron now flows in from above, and winds through the valley. Our path stretches over the hillside, and we enjoy the beautiful views of Mount Zion in the distance, which the Psalmist describes, 'Beautiful for situation, the joy of the whole earth is Mount Zion, *on the sides of the north.* Viewed from this point in the morning sunlight, Zion rising majestically on the north, seemed worthy of the fullest praises of David's harp.

"The country around presents a pastoral scene, and reminds us of patriarchal days. Sheep and goats are feeding upon the hillsides, and the shepherds' tents are pitched in the valleys. The road, however, is not entirely free from danger of attack. An armed Bedouin sheik accompanies us as guide and escort on our journey. In a short time we come to an encampment of black tents. Several armed men mount their horses as we approach, and much alarm is excited in our party. But they prove to be government soldiers in search of robbers, looking more like the robbers themselves, of whom they are in pursuit. They gallop around in Arab style, and make many warlike demonstrations, as they cross over the mountain.

"We now come to a vast gorge winding through the rock, several hundred feet deep, wild and grand beyond description. At the end of this natural chasm stands the rock-built convent of St. Saba, on the borders of the wilderness of Judea. Here a company of forty or fifty Greek monks spend their time in watching, fasting, and prayer. A more desolate and dreary spot could scarcely have been selected. The walls are built high and strong around to guard against the attacks of the Arabs; for the monastery is possessed of immense wealth, the gift of pious pilgrims. They let down a basket from an upper window to receive and examine our letters of introduction, and then admit us through a heavy iron door below. We visited the church, rich with paintings, golden crowns, and gold and silver lamps, where vespers are chanted every evening by the monks. The principal then conducts us to a side chapel, in a cave, wherein are gathered 14,000 skulls of Christians, slain by the Moslems in the Holy Land. Afterwards he points out to us the primitive cave which St. Saba entered when he came here to found the convent. It was inhabited by a lion, but the saint ordered him to retire, which he did at once, and faithfully kept guard fourteen years at the entrance of the cave. The rough walls are covered over with the crosses of pilgrims who have travelled here from afar, and fully believe the story.

" He also opened for us the chapel tomb of the saint. This is hung around with pictures of his prayers and miracles. One of these represents a pillar of cloud showing him the place to found his convent, a gazelle directing him where to find water, and the lion pointing out a place of safety. There are several small gardens in the grounds of the monastery, and one tall palm tree, planted, it is said, by the hand of St. Saba. The rooms for the entertainment of visitors appeared neat and comfortable, and we would gladly have spent the night within the walls. But there was a lady in our party, and the monks resolutely refused to grant her admittance, saying, 'if they did so, an earthquake would shake down the monastery, and there would be a famine for a year throughout the land.'

"We were accordingly obliged to remain in our tents; and there, commending ourselves to the protection of God, we slept peacefully through the night, awaked only by the ringing of the convent bell that summoned the monks to their midnight prayers.

"In the morning our friends of the monastery manifested their hospitality by bringing us bread, dates, and cheeses, as is the oriental custom, and we gave them of our stores, in return. Two Bedouin sheiks now join us as an escort on the journey, and we set out for the Dead Sea. Our path winds up the mountain side, and from the summit we have a commanding view over the Sand Mountains, even to the wilderness of Engedi, where David fled from the pursuit of Saul, 'among the rocks of the wild goats.' The mountains rise around like Alpine summits, clothed down their side with verdure, where sheep, goats, and camels are feeding. The Arabs point out the tomb of Moses on our left, and yonder stretch the dark waters of the sea in front. Descending thence, and crossing a small plain covered with stinted shrubs, we came to the shores of the Dead Sea. Nothing can equal the aspect of desolation that reigns around, showing the terrible convulsion of nature that manifested the wrath of God from heaven, in overthrowing the wicked cities of the plain. The mountains give evidence of volcanic irruption. No fish swim in the waters of the sea; no wild fowl float upon its surface; no living animal inhabits its shore. All is solitude and death. The water is of a dark-green color, and exceedingly acrid and bitter to the taste. We tested its peculiar buoyant qualities by the experiment of a bath. It was well nigh impossible to sink. We found that we could stand, sit, or lie in any position without the least effort. Indeed, I was surprised to find that I could walk erect in the water without reaching the bottom. We experienced no particular inconvenience from bathing, except an adhesive oily deposit left upon the skin, and to those who were unfortunately submerged, a most disagreeable, irritating effect in the throat and head.

"But we must not remain long in this burning sun and heated air. We soon mounted our horses and rode across the barren, salt-crusted plain to the banks of the Jordan. In a half hour from the sea we arrived at the bathing-place of the Pilgrims.

"There is scarcely any spot in Palestine I had so longed to visit as this upon the river Jordan. It is so interwoven in our hymns and sacred poetry with the borders of the promised land, the heavenly inheritance, that we seemed in a peculiar sense to be standing on the confines of a better land above.

"Here the children of Israel, following the ark of God, passed over on dry ground. 'The waters which came down from above stood and rose up upon an heap, and those that came down toward the sea of the plain (even the Salt Sea) failed and were cut off; and the people passed over right against Jericho.' Here Elijah and Elisha came and stood beside Jordan. 'And the prophet took his mantle and wrapped it together, and smote the waters, and they were divided hither and thither, so that they two went over on dry ground.' And just beyond, Elijah was caught up with 'a chariot of fire and horses of fire, and ascended by a whirlwind unto heaven.' Here also came Jesus to Jordan unto John, to be baptized of him. 'And Jesus when he was baptized went up straightway out of the water; and lo the heavens were opened unto him, and he saw the Spirit of God descending like a dove and lighting upon him, and lo a voice from heaven, saying: This is my beloved son in whom I am well pleased.' As we stood thus on the banks of Jordan, at the hour of sunset, these scenes all passed vividly before the mind, and we realized as never before their divine reality and power.

"Then two men came down to cross the river.

One passed firmly over, but the other, an aged man, trembled in the centre of the current, and his companion returned to his assistance and conducted him safely to the opposite shore. This also reminded us of the angel coming to strengthen the trembling pilgrim, as he crosses the dark river, and guide him triumphantly to the gates of the celestial city.

"We bathed in the rapid flowing waters, gathered a few mementos from the shore, and then unwillingly departed for our tents near the site of the ancient Jericho. I shall long remember that hallowed hour on the banks of the river Jordan.

"We rode from the Jordan across the plains of Jericho, at the hour of sunset and twilight. The valley is well watered, covered with wild flowers in full bloom, and, uncultivated by the hand of man, is still the garden of the Lord. Behind us, rising above the other peaks, is 'Mount Nebo, at the top of Pisgah,' where Moses, just before his death, went up from the plains of Moab. 'And the Lord showed him all the land of Gilead, and all the land of Judah, and the South, and the plain of the valley of Jericho, the city of palm trees, unto Zoar.' This view of the promised land, spread out like a Paradise before him, must have been lovely beyond description to the inspired lawgiver, whose 'eye was undimmed and his natural force unabated.' How beautiful an emblem, too, is it of the last hours of the faithful Christian, who is summoned to die upon the earthly mount of vision, with the heavenly world full in view; and angel messengers are waiting around, as for Elijah of old, to bear his triumphant spirit swift to the glories of the New Jerusalem.

"As we are thus enjoying the landscape and contemplating these scenes, we suddenly find that we have wandered from our path. And it becomes a matter of no slight anxiety, as we are unguarded among these hostile tribes. Evening came on apace, darkness gathered around us, and the lights from the Bedouin watchfires gleamed out from the mountain side.

"Our dragoman shouts and sounds his whistle, but no answer is returned. At length we fired a signal gun, and were rejoiced to hear the echo come back from our tents in the distance. We hastened thither, and found them pitched near the ruins of the ancient Jericho. As we drew near we were met by a company of women from a neighboring village, who had seen the American flag floating from the tents, and hearing that a Sultana would arrive, had come to greet the lady of our party (Mrs. Prime) with a welcome song. It was truly a remarkable specimen of native melody. They also demanded a backshish, and at the same time insisted upon being admitted to the tent that they might see the unveiled face of their fair sister. Thus gratified, they retired and left us undisturbed for the night.

"In the morning we walked out to search for traces of ancient Jericho, and discovered the remains of an old fountain and finely wrought mosaic pavement, indicating that a city of some magnificence had formerly occupied this site. An old dilapidated ruin is also pointed out as the house of Zaccheus where 'our Saviour abode with him and brought salvation to his house,' when he passed through Jericho. We then set out to visit the fountain of Elisha, a half hour distant. It bursts forth from underneath a large mound at the base of the mountain, and is a beautiful fountain of sweet and pleasant water. Its stream produces vegetation and flowers in luxuriant abundance as it flows over the plain. Originally the water was quite unfit for domestic purposes or irrigation, causing death and sterility, until the fountain was miraculously healed by the prophet Elisha, who 'went forth unto the spring of the waters and cast salt there, and said, Thus saith the Lord, I have healed these waters: there shall not be from thence any more death or barren land.'

"Thus according to the word of the Lord, it possesses peculiar virtue in producing vegetation, and spreads fertility and verdure over the plain, well nigh as far as the eye can reach. Indeed as the waters were bubbling forth, the birds singing in the trees, and many wild flowers were in bloom around, it seemed quite like an earthly paradise. We were then viewing the scene of a perpetual miracle, reaching from the days of Elisha to the present, and yielding to these deadly waters a life-giving power to make the barren land bloom with beauty and rejoice as the garden of the Lord. I could not but feel that it was greatly fitted to confirm and strengthen our faith in the miracles of Scripture history.

"Then we rode along the base of Mount Quarantana, a bold and precipitous peak that rises twelve or fifteen hundred feet above the plain. This is described as the point where 'Jesus was led up of the Spirit into the wilderness to be tempted of the devil,' and when he had successfully resisted the assaults of the Evil One, 'behold angels came and ministered unto him.' The mountain side is filled with grottoes and caves cut in the rock, the dwelling-places of pious monks who formerly fled here from the temptations of the world. They found, however, that the old tempter was in this wilderness, still seeking whom he might destroy, and that we must escape the world before we can escape the wiles of the adversary.

"Next we came to a wild rocky ravine that opens through the mountain. Down this the brook Cherith winds its way to the valley, and here the prophet Elijah 'hid himself at the command of the Lord by the brook Cherith, that is before Jordan.' 'And the ravens brought him bread and flesh in the morning, and bread and flesh in the evening; and he drank of the brook.' We were thus viewing the scene of another miracle of Bible history, and felt the presence of the God of Elijah beside the waters of the brook Cherith. An old monk has cut his cell high up in the rock, and dwelt there in imitation of the prophet. Ascending thence by an ancient paved road, we reach the mountain summit and take our last view of the valley of the Jordan, the Dead Sea, and the mountains round about. On the way the place is pointed out where 'a certain man going down from Jerusalem to Jericho fell among thieves, and the good Samaritan had compassion on him, and set him on his own beast, and brought him to an inn.' The road here certainly appears as though it had always been infested with thieves and robbers, and on this account was doubtless selected as the scene of the parable. Four armed Bedouins now came suddenly upon us in the pass, and we at first feared the fate of the former traveller. We, however, made the salutation of friendship to them, and they immediately returned it and acted as our guard by the way. Thence we came to Bethany, and crossing the Mount of Olives, entered once more within the Holy City."

CHAPTER XVIII.

FROM JERUSALEM TO DAMASCUS.

MR. RIGHTER left Jerusalem March 10th, having on the same morning met a number of Christian friends at Bishop Gobat's study, and having persuaded them to form a Committee of the Evangelical Alliance with Bishop Gobat as Chairman He gives the following account of his journey to Damascus:

"BEYROOT, April 8, 1856.

"From Jerusalem we journeyed northward, and came to Bethel, or, House of God, where Jacob saw in his dream a ladder set upon the earth, and the top of it reached to heaven, and behold the angels of God ascended and descended upon it, and behold the Lord stood above it, and said: 'I am the Lord God of Abraham, thy father, and the God of Isaac: the land whereon thou liest, to thee will I give it, and to thy seed. . And Jacob awaked out of his sleep, and he was afraid and said, How dreadful is this place! this is none other but the house of God, and this is the gate of heaven . . . And he called the name of that place Bethel.'

"Passing by way of Shiloh, where the ark and tabernacle long continued, we next arrived at Nablous, the ancient Shechem. Near by is Jacob's well, where our Saviour sat wearied with his journey, and as the woman of Samaria came to draw water, he discoursed to her of the water of everlasting life. On the right rises Ebal, the Mount of Cursing, and on the left Gerizim, the Mount of Blessing, whereon the Samaritans built a temple and worshipped God, in opposition to the Jews at Jerusalem. And here the small remnant that is left still go up four times a year to offer sacrifice and worship. They live entirely distinct; and as of old, 'the Jews have no dealings with the Samaritans.'

"In the morning we ascended an eminence, and, looking to the east, saw Ramothgilead beyond Jordan, where Moses set before the Israelites 'a blessing and a curse,' and charged them to place the blessing upon Mount Gerizim, and the curse upon Mount Ebal. 'Are they not on the other side Jordan, by the way where the sun goeth down, in the land of the Canaanites?' This Joshua afterward did, when they entered in to possess the land, placing 'half of them over against Mount Gerizim, and half of them over against Mount Ebal,' as Moses, the servant of the

Lord, had commanded before. 'And he read all the words of the law, the blessings and the cursings, according to all that is written in the book of the law.' And all the people answered Amen. It was most interesting to view and realize this whole scene, spread out like a picture before us.

"We then journeyed on, and in half an hour came to the hill of Samaria. Here stood Herod's ivory palace, and this sensual monarch reigned in all his ambitious splendor. Here the daughter of Herodias, Herod's brother's wife, danced before him on his birthday, and pleased Herod. Whereupon he promised to give her whatsoever she would ask, even to the half of his kingdom: and at her request Herod sent, and beheaded John in prison, and his head was brought in a charger, and given to the damsel. More than sixty massive columns, that formed the long colonnade in front of Herod's palace, are still standing on the hillside of Samaria. Thence, crossing the great plain of Esdraelon, and ascending the steep hill side that bounds it on the north, we came to the town of Nazareth. It is beautifully situated in a basin, encompassed by hills that command a fine view of the country round. Here the angel Gabriel was sent from God to predict unto Mary the birth of an infant Saviour, 'who should be called great, the Son of the Highest. And the Lord God shall give unto him the throne of his father David, and he shall reign over the house of Jacob for ever, and of his kingdom there shall be no end.' The fountain is near by, where it is said the annunciation was made by the divine messenger.. After the flight into Egypt, we read that 'Joseph,' being warned of God in a dream that Herod was dead, 'arose, and took the young child and his mother, and came and dwelt in a city called Nazareth; that it might be fulfilled which was spoken by the prophets, He shall be called a Nazarene.' Here our Saviour spent nearly thirty years of his life, and these scenes were all familiar to him. To Nazareth also he first came after his baptism and temptation, and entered into the synagogue on the Sabbath day, and from the book of the prophet Esaias preached the acceptable year of the Lord.

"There are two missionaries of the English Church Missionary Society established here. They have a school numbering forty-one children, of whom thirty are Protestants, six Greeks, four Latins, and one Armenian. The Scriptures in the Old and New Testaments are used as a textbook. During the last year fifteen Bibles in Arabic and six in Italian have been sold and distributed among the people. They have now decided, however, to confine themselves entirely to the sale of Scriptures, and no longer give them gratuitously as heretofore. Since, about twenty

Arabic Bibles have recently been collected in the convent, and burned by the Catholic priests. As the leaves were crackling in the flames, they shouted, 'This is the voice of the devil.' Notwithstanding, there is an increased desire for the Scriptures among all classes. Even the Catholics would have the Bible, but for the prohibition of the priests. Nazareth has a population of about 4,500, as follows: Moslems, 2,300; Greeks, 1,000; Latins, 500; Maronites, 200; Greek Catholics, 250; Protestants, 100.

"We set out on our journey the next day, crossing the summit of Mount Tabor, and in the evening arrived at Tiberias, on the Sea of Galilee.

"This was, to me, one of the most interesting localities in the Holy Land. Around these shores the Saviour loved to dwell, and here most of his mighty works were done. Simon Peter, and Andrew his brother, James the son of Zebedee, and John his brother, were fishermen of this sea, and were called thence by our Saviour to follow him. On this lake he came walking to them on the water; and here, when the winds and waves arose, he stilled the tempest with his word, saying, 'Peace, be still;' and suddenly there was a great calm. On a mountain near by he miraculously fed the multitude of 4,000 men with 'seven loaves and a few little fishes;' and upon another delivered his sermon on the mount to his disciples.

Here stood Capernaum, Chorazin, and Bethsaida, whose terrible overthrow the Saviour predicted because of their unbelief, and their ruined sites only remain to attest the truth of his prophecy. We spent a delightful Sabbath on the shores of the Sea of Galilee, and joined in the worship of our Divine Redeemer, who walked here clothed in humanity. Tiberias is one of the holy cities of the Jews, and they are miserable and bigoted in the extreme. No missionary lives among them, and no Scriptures have been distributed. I called upon a Greek priest, and had a pleasant interview. He wished a few copies of the Scriptures for his people.

"In two days more across the hills and along the valley of the Jordan, we came to Banias, the ancient Cesarea Philippi. Here we traced the last footsteps of our Saviour in the north of Palestine. It was pleasant, also, to leave the Holy Land with the scene of the transfiguration impressed last upon the mind; for it was doubtless upon one of these mountains near by that this sublime event occurred. 'When Jesus came into the coasts of Cesarea Philippi, he asked his disciples, Whom do men say that I, the son of man, am?' 'Then he showed unto his disciples that he must go unto Jerusalem, and suffer many things of the elders and chief priests and scribes, and be killed, and be raised again the third day;'

and he also spake of his coming 'in the glory of his Father, with his angels; and then he shall reward every man according to his works.' Immediately following this conversation as related by Matthew, it is said: 'And after six days Jesus taketh Peter, James, and John his brother, and bringeth them up into a high mountain apart, and was transfigured before them: and his face did shine as the sun, and his raiment was white as the light. And, behold, there appeared unto them Moses and Elias talking with him. . . . Behold, a bright cloud overshadowed them: and behold a voice out of the cloud, which said, This is my beloved Son, in whom I am well pleased: hear ye him.' Such was our last view of the Saviour in the Holy Land—transfigured, glorified, as he will come again to judge the world, and bring his redeemed ones to reign with him in heaven.

"Then we crossed the Anti-Lebanon range of mountains, and in two days more reached Damascus. Here I met with two missionaries of the Irish Presbyterian Church, the Rev. Messrs. Robeson and Porter, and three American missionaries of the Associate Reformed Presbyterian Church, Dr. Paulding and the Rev. Messrs. Frazer and Lansing. They are laboring harmoniously, side by side, in the same field, to spread the Bible and preach the Gospel among the vast multitudes of this city. Miss Dales of Philadelphia, is also associated with them in the missionary work. Damascus is said to contain a population of 125,000; viz. Moslems, 100,000; Greeks (speaking Arabic), 8,000; Jews, 5,000; Greek Catholics, 8,000; and a few Armenians, Maronites, Druses, and Syrians.

"There have been sold during the last year 259 Arabic Scriptures, and thirty-seven copies in Hebrew, Turkish, and English. The school for boys numbers thirty-seven, principally from the Greeks. I was much gratified in attending a Bible class of Greek boys instructed by the Rev. Mr. Porter. He examined them in their regular course of lessons on the seventeenth and eighteenth chapters of Isaiah, upon the subject of the burden of Damascus and Egypt. They appeared very intelligent and much interested in the Scriptures. I also visited the girls' school under the charge of Miss Dales: they repeated portions of the Psalms and New Testament very readily and well, and seemed delighted to study their lessons from the Bible. The Greek Patriarch has also a large school, in which the Scriptures are taught. I called upon him in behalf of the Bible cause, and he appeared much interested to hear of the Bible work and the progress of religious liberty at Constantinople.

"There is a new interest with regard to the

Scriptures springing up at Damascus. A resolution was taken at their last station meeting to establish a Bible dépôt in the principal street of the city. This surely is encouraging in the ancient stronghold of Moslem intolerance and fanaticism.

"Returning by way of Baalbeck, the ancient temple of Baal, I arrived at Beyroot in time to attend the annual meeting of the Syrian mission, and present the subject of the Bible interests before the brethren of all the stations assembled in their general council. They gave me a very kind reception, and assigned a special hour for listening to statements respecting the Bible work at Constantinople, in Egypt, Palestine, and Syria. They also, on their part, presented encouraging reports from each of their fields of labor.

"The population to which their missionary effort is directed, in the towns and villages on and around Mount Lebanon, consists of the following classes: Moslems, 51,000; Greeks, 45,500; Maronites, 24,000; Druses, 15,500. Their principal success, however, is attained among the Greeks. They have established Protestant schools at the different stations, in which 550 boys and 250 girls are taught the Scriptures.

"There have been distributed and sold by this mission during the last year, 532 Arabic Scriptures, five Turkish, nine Hebrew, and two Syriac. The American Bible Society have in press at Beyroot a new and complete translation of the whole Bible in Arabic, by the Rev. Dr. Eli Smith. The printing of the Old Testament with references has proceeded as far as Exodus, and the New as far as the eighth chapter of Matthew. The work must necessarily progress slowly by reason of the extreme accuracy of the translator and editor. Dr. Smith gave me the following account of the thorough system he pursues with regard to it:

"The translation is first made directly from the original by one of the native helpers, to give the style of the Arabic. This Dr. Smith works over with all the critical assistance of books he can command. He then calls in another native helper, and they criticise together. A fair copy of this is made. He then goes over the whole *de novo* with the assistance of a third native helper; after which another copy is transcribed, and the work is put in press. Twenty or thirty proofs of this are struck off, and sent to the bishop of Jerusalem, to Cairo, Damascus, to all the stations in Syria, and several natives for examination. By this means the translator learns what words or phrases may not be understood in any of the sectional dialects. In twenty or thirty days these proofs are all received, their suggestions examined, and a corrected copy prepared for printing. Two important points are thus gained—the correctness of the version, and the approbation of all the different societies concerned. The Arabic, like other Eastern languages, has both a classic usage and modern dialect. The doctor follows the classic style in language and grammar, but only so far as it is intelligible to the common people. It will, consequently, be understood by the immense Arabic-speaking population of Syria, Egypt, Mosul, Bagdad, and India.

"He places various readings in the margin, as in the English version. Such is the carefully elaborate and accurate system pursued, to make this the most perfect translation of the Bible in any language in the world. The first translation has already been made of the Pentateuch, the seven minor prophets, and the entire New Testament. It will, however, require five or six years to complete the whole at the present rate of progress. Yet the demand is so urgent, that a resolution has been taken to suspend for the present the Old, and hasten forward the New Testament as fast as possible. I deeply regret to inform our Board that the health of Dr. Smith is very much impaired by his arduous labors, so that he will be obliged to discontinue his duties for the summer. The earnest prayer of all is that he may be speedily restored and spared, by the blessing of God, to complete this great work of his life.

"I also had the pleasure of meeting with my excellent predecessor, the Rev. S. H. Calhoun, at

Beyroot, and conferring with him in regard to the Bible work. He sends his kind remembrance to all his old friends.

"My visit to Egypt, Palestine, and Syria, has thus been of the greatest interest, and I trust will be productive of the most lasting and important results in behalf of the Bible Cause in the East."

"Affectionately, yours,

"C. N. RIGHTER."

On Thursday, April 19, he notes in his journal, "In sight of the domes and minarets of Stamboul, and thankful for a safe return from a long and happy journey."

The spring and summer were spent at Constantinople in the work of Bible distribution, and in laying and carrying out his plans for spreading it over the East. He visited the hospitals as before, taking with him the word of life for the poor soldiers. There was no difficulty in gaining access to them, and his visits were most gratefully received. On one of these occasions he accompanied the philanthropist, Miss Dix, who was then in the East, on her mission of mercy to the asylums of the unfortunate. During the month of August he had an attack of fever which confined him to his room for many days, and prevented much active service during the month. The physician pronounced the seat of his disease to be his liver, and it is impossible to say what connexion it may have had with his subsequent fatal illness.

During all his residence at Constantinople his intercourse with the missionaries was a source of the highest mutual pleasure, and his relations to the Hon. Mr. Spence, Minister from the United States to Turkey, were of the most friendly and agreeable character, as will appear from the letters which will be found in the concluding part of this volume, and which bear the highest testimony to Mr. Righter's worth, and to the estimation in which he was held.

CHAPTER XIX.

JOURNEY TO NINEVEH.

On the first of September he became acquainted with the Rev. Mr. Jones, Secretary of the Turkish Missions Aid Society, who was about to visit the interior stations of Asia Minor. Mr. R. almost immediately determined on joining him in furtherance of the great object which had called him to the East. Accordingly he made his arrangements for the departure, which, owing to the detention of the vessel, was deferred until the 16th. In the meanwhile he mentions in his journal, under date of September 14, attending at Pera the baptism of the first Christian Mohammedan child, Henry Julius Williams, by Rev. Dr. Goodell, at the chapel of the Dutch Embassy, as an occasion of deep interest. He took his departure from Constantinople for the last time, as it afterwards appeared, September 16th. A beautiful rainbow marked the morning on which he set sail, and hastily bidding his friends farewell, he went on board the steamer Imperial Eagle, with the Rev. Mr. Jones.

Mr. R. gives the following account of his journey:

"We left Constantinople on the 16th and sailed two days across the Black Sea to Samsoun upon the coast. Here we took horses and rode three days to Marsovan, for several years a missionary station of the American Board. The Protestant pastor, Hohanes, and one of the native brethren came out to meet us two hours before our arrival, and gave us a cordial welcome. And as we reached the city, many Armenians hastened to give us their salutations as brethren in Christ. It was most pleasant to be thus kindly welcomed as Christians in a strange land.

"In the evening a special meeting was held, and I stated to them the object of my visit—to furnish the Bible in every language to all who desired it in the East. They expressed their thankfulness very sincerely, and wished me to convey their gratitude to the American Bible Society for giving them the pure Bible and Gospel in the modern Armenian language, which all can understand, that each one for himself may read God's Word and be instructed in the way of everlasting salvation. The next day I visited the book-store, near the bazaar, in the central street of the city. Here the Scriptures are publicly kept for sale in Armenian, Turkish, and Greek. There have been sold during the last year, twenty-four Armenian and eleven Greek Bibles and Testaments. The demand for the Scriptures is also increasing. I received an order for the following: Sixty Græco-Turkish Testaments; twenty Turkish Bibles; twenty Turkish Psalms; thirty large Armenian Bibles; thirty Armenian Testaments; forty Armeno-Turkish Testaments, making 200 copies of the Scriptures for the ensuing year. We then visited the Protestant school, which numbers forty children. We found them reading and studying the Scriptures. At morning and evening prayer also, the Old and New Testaments are read and explained. I likewise made a visit to the native Armenian school. The teacher received me very politely, said he had the Bible and Gospel in the Armenian language, which he taught daily to his pupils; and also, that he desired an additional supply.

"We afterwards enjoyed a very interesting visit with a sheik or chief of a sect of Dervishes (Mohammedan monks), who have a convent near Marsovan, to which many pilgrims resort. He received us very politely in his library room, and first presented his little boy to us, in token of mutual friendship. He says he has the Bible and Testament, and has carefully read and studied both. He himself copied the gospel of Matthew in manuscript several years since. He borrowed it by night from a friendly Turk in the seraglio, wrote it as he could, and returned it in the day-time for fear of discovery. I asked him, 'What is your opinion of the Bible?' Said he, 'It would take me two days to tell you. The Word of God is everlasting. You cannot cut it, cannot burn it, cannot destroy it. It is in the world for ever. It teaches Christ, the Gospel of love—love to God and love to man. In Jesus we love one another as brothers. There are three kinds of love: first, common friendship; second, to lay down one's life for his friends; third, to love your enemies. All these are taught in the Bible. There is a hidden treasure in the gospel that will be brought to light more and more in coming time, till it is known and prized by all the world.' I told him that many Mussulmen in Constantinople are at present seeking for the Bible and valuing it much, and we hope soon all will have it. He replied, 'I must not speak publicly my sentiments now, or my head will be taken off at once.' It was most gratifying to find him so enlightened and imbued with the spirit and love of the Gospel. He says, 'I love the gospel of John, the beloved disciple, who fully unfolds the tender love of Jesus. That iron yonder is cold, but when you put it in the fire it becomes warm and heated. So when we come together we may be strangers at first, but our hearts soon grow warm with the love of Christ.' And as we came to separate he embraced and kissed us affectionately, and with tears in his eyes expressed the hope that we might meet in heaven. He is but one of a large class of Mussulmen in the East who are becoming enlightened by studying the Scriptures, but are kept from embracing Christianity through fear of persecution and death.

"In a town named Soungoloo, twenty hours distant from Marsovan, a hojah, or Turkish teacher, not long since became possessed of a copy of the Scriptures. He continued to study it with much interest, and then began to explain it to others; and now, it is said, as many as one thousand are interested in seeking after the truth. As we left Marsovan, the pastor, the children, and the native brethren accompanied us some distance on our journey, and then took leave of us with much thankfulness and gratitude for our visit in behalf of the Gospel and the Bible Cause. We arrived the same day at Amasia. Here I called upon the Armenian archbishop, and stated to him the object of my mission—to furnish all, who desire it, with the Word of God, without note or comment. He received me with great politeness, but said that all his people were supplied with the Scriptures.

"In two days more we reached Tocat, and were again welcomed by a delegation of the missionaries and the native brethren an hour before our arrival in the city. This is in many respects the most important interior station of the mission. The Rev. Mr. Van Lennep has here a theological seminary, in which ten pious young men are preparing to preach the Gospel. In vacations they go out into all the towns and villages round about and labor as Bible colporteurs and Scripture readers among the native population. In a city ten hours distant they remained up all night, on one occasion, in arguing from the Scriptures and establishing the truth by the Word of God.

The next day is the Sabbath, and I was much interested in attending their native services in Armenian and Turkish. In the evening a special meeting was called, and I explained to them the object of my visit, and the desire of the American Bible Society to aid in supplying the Scriptures in all the languages of the East. I also gave them an account of my visit to the soldiers in the Crimea, to the Copts in Egypt, and of my journey in Palestine and Syria. They were deeply interested, and desired me to thank 'that great and good Society for remembering also the Armenians in Asia Minor.' The Protestant Church numbers twenty-five members, and the congregation usually from forty to sixty. There is also a Sabbath school and day school, in which the Scriptures are taught to the children. The next day I visited the Bible dépôt, a large room in the principal street of the city. There have been sold during the last year, ninety-seven copies of the Scriptures and parts of Scriptures in Armenian, Greek, and Turkish. One hundred and ninety-three copies have also been distributed by the colporteurs in the city, and the towns, and villages around. Here, likewise, the demand is increasing: two hundred additional copies have just been ordered from Constantinople to supply the depository.

"In the afternoon I made a visit to the grave of Henry Martin, who died at Tocat, in 1812. It was most interesting to stand beside the tomb of that devoted missionary, who 'labored so many years in the East, and translated the Holy Scriptures into Hindostanee and Persian.' The East India Company are about to erect an elegant monument to his memory, in the grounds of the American mission, where his remains will be removed and deposited. I have just held an interview, this evening, with a converted Mussulman from Aintab. He obtained a copy of the New Testament at Beyroot some years ago, became convinced of the truth of the Gospel, and has since distributed more than one hundred copies among the Kuzul Bashis Koords and Turks around Arabkir. He has changed his name from Mohammed to Kreker, or Gregory, and gone into all the towns and villages of that region, everywhere preaching the Word. I inquired his opinion of the Bible. 'I believe it to be the Word of God,' said he; 'and Christ is the Son of God, who took upon himself our nature to save sinners. This he did by his atonement and resurrection, and afterward he sent his Holy Spirit to renew us unto newness of life.' I asked him whence he obtained this knowledge? He replied, 'By studying the Scriptures alone.' Such is the power of the simple Word of God, to make even a follower of the false prophet wise unto everlasting salvation.

"He is now on his way to Constantinople, to be baptized and fully embrace the Christian religion.

"Faithfully and affectionately yours,

"C. N. RIGHTER."

In a letter to his mother he speaks of his visit to the grave of Henry Martin, in a manner which shows that he was not unprepared in thought to find an early grave near this precious dust. There is something deeply touching and almost prophetic in the thoughts which he expressed on visiting this spot.

"TOCAT, Oct. 2, 1856.

"I am now upon a journey to the interior stations of the Armenian Missions in Asia Minor, and have time this morning only to write a hasty note from this most interesting place. Here Henry Martin lies buried—that devoted missionary in the East, who in India translated the Holy Scriptures into Hindostanee and Persian, and died with fever at Tocat, on his journey to Constantinople. I have this afternoon made a visit to his grave. It was just at the hour of sunset. A mild and mellow light was shed over the scene, and I could not but feel my devotion quickened, and faith strengthened beside the last resting-place of this man of God, cut off in early manhood, in the midst of his active labors, in a far distant land. Again a voice came to me—'What thy hand findeth to do, do it with thy might, for in such an hour as ye think not the Son of Man cometh.'

"Tocat is beautifully situated at the head of a fertile valley, abounding in gardens, vineyards, and fruit-trees of most luxuriant growth. The missionary brethren came out to welcome us in the name of Christ; and after we had spent a few days with them in delightful Christian intercourse, sent us on our way rejoicing. My travelling companion is the Rev. Henry Jones, secretary of the Turkish Missions Aid Society, a man of devoted piety, and an excellent Christian gentleman. Our object is to visit all the missionary stations in Asia Minor, to witness the work of the Lord in connexion with the Bible cause, and the cause of missions, and to establish a branch of the Evangelical Alliance as far as may be practicable at each station.

"From Tocat we traversed the bold and rugged mountains, constantly viewing picturesque and beautiful scenery, and in two days came to Sivas, a second missionary station of the American Board. We were somewhat alarmed by the reported attacks of robbers by the way, but through the good providence of God, arrived in safety. The missionaries and native brethren came out on horseback, two hours in advance, to give us a cordial welcome. Indeed our whole journey seems more like Pilgrim's Progress than any I have ever yet made. The land is beautiful, and the climate most delightful. Though there are occasional perils and dangers in the way, yet all is 'the King's country,' and must one day be converted to Christ. At each station, too, we hold such sweet communion and fellowship with our Christian brethren in this far off land, as can only dwell in kindred hearts. We are entertained in the 'palace called Beautiful,' and sleep in the 'chamber of Peace,' as at times we repose two or three days from the fatigues of our journey. Here, in Sivas, we administered the communion of the Lord's supper to the little church gathered in the name of Christ, and we did indeed sit together in heavenly places in

Christ Jesus, with his elect ones in this Moslem land. On the morrow we went on our way, escorted by our good friends some distance on the plain, where we parted, commending each other to the blessing of heaven in all our labors.

"In six days, over mountains, through winding valleys and extended plains, we reached the missionary station of Arabkir, in the borders of the ancient Cappadocia. It is a city of gardens in the midst of the mountains, and exceedingly beautiful for situation. Here we were received again by warm Christian hearts, and rejoiced to witness their good work, and cheer them in their arduous labors.

"We also joined in celebrating the communion with them and their native church, and much enjoyed the season. The hearts of the native converts are overflowing with love and gratitude to those who have sent to them the Bible and missionaries of the gospel of Christ. They crowd around us, and shake our hands with tears in their eyes.

"Again we pursued our journey, and at the close of the day came down to the river Euphrates, one of the four rivers that flowed from the Garden of Eden. It runs here with a swift current, through a narrow gorge in the mountains—a broad and noble stream. And inspiring indeed were my first impressions in looking upon this ancient river that flowed from the paradise of our first parents.

"Crossing the Euphrates, we spent the night at the town of Maden, on the opposite bank. Here also we joined in a social prayer meeting with the little Protestant church that has received the pure faith of the gospel through the labors of the American missionaries. They were delighted to be assured that we in England and America believed the same Bible and gospel with them, and that we could hold fellowship together in the name of a common Saviour.

"The next morning we rode on our journey (we travel entirely on horseback in this land; there are no roads for carriages, only mountain foot and bridle paths), and came to *Kharpoot*, situated on a fortress rock that commands a splendid view over a wide extended plain. This is one of the more recent missionary stations, and no church had yet been formed. Our visit was considered a favor able occasion for organizing a church, and we were glad to assist in examining the candidates, and admitting them as members of the church of Christ. One of them was the father of a family, with his young daughter, and another a converted Armenian priest, who seemed to receive the truth anew with full simplicity and sincerity of heart.

"The next day we continued our journey over the plain, and across the rugged mountains, and in three days reached *Diarbekir*, a large walled city, situated at the head waters of the Tigris, on the borders of the plains of Mesopotamia. We spent another delightful Sabbath with the native and missionary brethren here, and held sweet communion and fellowship together. One of the latter was an old friend of mine in college, and we enjoyed much our visit in the recollection of former scenes, and in relating our various experience since we separated.

"The climate is mild and genial at this season, and the scenery varied and picturesque. Through the kindness of the American Ambassador at Constantinople, I have a large firman from the Sultan, bearing his great seal, which secures us the particular attention and entertainment of all the Pashas and Governors on the way, so that we are exceedingly enjoying the tour. In addition to this, we are cheered in our visit and encouraged in our labors at each station, and thus go forward rejoicing in the Lord, and giving thanks at the remembrance of his holiness.

"On the following day we took our departure for Mosul. We are now mounted on a raft of a hundred inflated goat skins, and glide beautifully down the Tigris, the Hiddekel of the Scriptures, another of the four rivers that flowed from the Garden of Eden; 'that is it which goeth toward the east of Assyria.' A neat little house of poplar poles covered with wax cloth, to protect us from the sun and rain, and fitted up with poplomans and lined within for our comfort. A guard of soldiers have volunteered to accompany us, free of expense, and sleep round us at night. Thus we float on with the current. It is the perfection of travelling without the rattling of wheels, without dust, without steam even. The stream floats us on night and day, and at intervals we whirl past rocks, and dash swiftly down the rapids. The mountains and rocks rise in grandeur and sublimity on either side, as the noble river winds its way through.

" We spent the Sabbath at Hassankeefa, a city hewn out in the solid rocks like Petra in the land of Edom. It is now crumbling to ruins, and the miserable population live in the tombs of the former dwellers in the rock. Yesterday we passed the river Chabur, the ancient Chebar, that comes down from the mountains of Chaldea, and flows into the Tigris. Here the Prophet Ezekiel saw his sublime visions in the land of the Chaldeans, by the river Chebar, when the heavens were opened and Jehovah manifested to him his peculiar presence and glory. I enjoyed anew these spiritual scenes as we gazed long upon the banks of that ancient river.

Nov. 9.—To-day at noon we are in sight of the walls and minarets of Mosul, and Nelly

Yonas, the tomb of the Prophet Jonah, that covers the ruins of the ancient Nineveh, 'that great city of three days journey.'

"Thus the Lord has protected and prospered us on our way, and followed us with goodness in all our journey. In the words of the Psalmist we would exclaim, 'Bless the Lord, our soul: and all that is within us, bless his holy name.'

"Yours, &c. C. N. R."

Below are given some of the incidents of the journey, communicated to the American Bible Society:

"As we left Tocat, Hagop Agha, the head of the Protestant community, and all the students of the seminary, in a body, accompanied us on our way to a hillside that overlooks the city. They then gathered around us in a circle, and we commended them to God and the Bible as their rule of faith, and the Guide of their lives, and exhorted them to show forth the light of the Gospel of Christ in this dark land, and be faithful unto death, that they might receive the crown of life at his right hand. One of their number, in return, thanked us cordially for our visit, and our societies for sending them the Bible and the Gospel of salvation, and prayed that the peace of God might abide with us on the journey, and the blessing of heaven rest upon all our labors in the

East. We then traversed a rugged, mountainous region, and in two days reached *Sivas*, a second missionary station of the American Board. The brethren, as before, came out on horseback, one hour in advance, to welcome us in the name of Christ. The city is beautifully situated upon an elevated plain between two ranges of limestone hills, with a stream of pure water flowing through. It contains a population of nearly 50,000; of whom 36,000 are Turks, 12,000 Armenians, and 300 Greeks. The Scriptures are kept publicly for sale at four different points in the city, and a new depository is about to be opened in front of the principal bazaar. There have been sold during the last year: Armenian Bibles, twenty-three; Testaments, thirty-five; Psalms, sixty-seven; Turkish Testaments, twenty-three; Græco-Turkish Testaments, ten; making 158 copies of Scriptures.

"They likewise wished a large additional supply for the coming year. I then called upon the Armenian bishop at the monastery. He is an amiable, venerable-looking man, and received me with the greatest politeness: 'Safa gueldùig; khos gueldùig;'—(You are welcome; most welcome). I explained to him the object of the American Bible Society—to furnish the Bible in all the languages of the East; stating, that 'in America, every family who desires it has a copy of the Bible; and American Christians desire that every family in the East may also receive the Word of God.' He says, 'This is a very good work. Every family of my people also has, or can have the Bible if they wish. They can receive it both in the ancient and modern languages.'

"This was regarded as a most important admission by an Armenian bishop in the presence of the missionaries—that the Bible should have free circulation among his people.

"In the afternoon a public meeting of the Protestant community was held at the mission chapel. The Rev. Mr. Jones, from England, addressed them in relation to his society, and I, from America, in behalf of the Bible Cause. They were greatly interested in the account of our new Bible House at New York, and all the operations of the Bible Society, of which they had never before heard. And it was most pleasing to receive their warm expressions of gratitude for thus receiving the Bible and the Gospel of Christ at our hands. The next day was the Sabbath. We attended service in the native languages, and then administered the communion of the Lord's Supper to the little church gathered here; and it was an occasion of deep interest to sit around the table of our Lord with these brethren in a strange land.

"In the afternoon, two of the Kuzelbash Koords, from a village twelve hours distant, called upon us. One is the son of the sheik, or chief man of the village. They expressed a desire to become Protestants, and embrace the Gospel of Christ. I asked them why they wished to change their religion. They replied: we formerly worshipped a cane, or staff, with which the sheik, or priest, beat us, to drive away our sins. We used to meet once a week and receive this beating, and repeat certain incantations. Then we confessed our sins to the sheik, and once a year offered a sacrifice of sheep to this cane. We no longer believe that this can save us. A kitab (good book) taught us better.'

"'Whence did you receive this Book?'

"'We know not,' they say. 'It teaches us that Christ is alive, and the other prophets are dead. It teaches us to love our enemies, and pray for them. It is ten years since we began to learn these truths.'

"'What is the name of this Book?'

"'We call it Boyurook' (book of authority or command), they answer. 'A khojah, or teacher, reads to us from this Book, the sheik explains it, and we then pray to God through Christ, as his Book teaches.'

"I tell them we also have the same Book in America, and call it 'Ingil" (Gospel of Salvation).

"They answer, 'We would be delighted to have a good missionary from America come and live among us, to instruct us in this way of salvation. We are called Protestants by the Koords, and our enemies beat us and drive away our flocks because we will not worship idols as they do.'

"We tell them they must expect to suffer persecution for believing in Christ; but if they are faithful, God will deliver them from the hand of their enemies; that they must return to their village, and preach this same Gospel of Love and Salvation even to their persecutors.

"'Inshallah' (God be praised)! they both exclaim. They tell us that 500 others are ready to receive the Gospel with them, but for fear of the savage Koords. We then promised to call and represent their case of persecution to the Turkish authorities, that they might enjoy liberty of conscience to believe in the Bible and Gospel of Christ, as the late firman of the Sultan declares to all the subjects of his empire. Such is the influence of a single unknown Testament, to teach these poor Kuzelbash, in the interior of Asia Minor, the folly of their idol worship, and lead them to believe in Christ as their only Saviour from sin. On the morrow we set out on our journey. The brethren accompanied us some distance on the plain, and then bade us farewell, commending our way to the Lord. We spent the night at the small Armenian village of Oolash. The priest and chourbagi (chief man of the village) called to see us, and the conversation soon turned upon the Bible and Testament. Our dragoman, who is a zealous Protestant, at once enlisted, and preached the Gospel to the little company for two hours with much earnestness. We trust that some fruit may spring from the good seed sown by the way in that quiet village. In another village where we passed the night, the moodir, or Turkish governor, inquired if we were travelling through the country to make all the people Protestants. We answered, that 'our object was to give the Bible and preach the Gospel to all who were willing to hear and receive it.' To our great surprise he replied, 'This is according to the Sultan's decree.' We were delighted thus to find that such liberal ideas were gradually penetrating into the interior of the empire.

"In four days more we reached Arabkir, a city of gardens in the midst of the mountains. It contains a population of 30,000, of whom 20,000 are Mussulmans, and 10,000 Armenians. There are also 300 enrolled in the Protestant community. This is a most important centre of missionary operations. Twenty-two native helpers are employed; of these, six are preachers, two are engaged at the Bible depôts, two are colporteurs, and twelve are teachers. All are more or less engaged in the work of circulating the Scriptures. There are six schools, containing one hundred pupils, in which the Bible and Testament are made the chief books of instruction. I also visited the Bible shop in the midst of the business bazaars of the city, and found there a large Armenian and Turkish Bible lying open, that any who passed by might read the Word of God. There have been disposed of from thence, within the last five months, eighteen Bibles and one hundred and three Testaments. I likewise visited two of the schools, and found the children diligently studying the Bible and Testament, and learning the way of salvation. Then I called upon the chief vartabed of the Armenian Church. He received me very cordially, and said, 'he taught all his people that they must have the Bible and read it. He had a copy of our Modern Armenian Bible, and would examine it, and if the translation were correct, he would at once recommend it to his people.' He was desirous also to have the Word circulated among the Kuzelbash. It was our duty to endeavor to enlighten and Christianize them. He wishes to preach only what is found in the Bible, and prays that Koords and Mussulmans may all receive the truth as it is in Jesus, and be made happy in the love of Christ.

"As I leave, he presses me warmly by the hand, and says, 'If we both live in the faith of the Gospel, we will meet again in heaven.' He seemed to be a man of excellent liberal spirit for a chief ecclesiastic in the Armenian Church.

"We afterward visited the school under his direction, and found a class of larger boys translating the Bible from the ancient to the modern language, which they can understand. The teacher says that ours is a correct translation, and does not differ from the ancient version. Thus the Bible is penetrating among the Armenians in their schools and families, and we trust will soon bring them from the darkness and deadness of superstition to the light and life of the Gospel of Christ. I was much interested in the experience of one of the native preachers. He first obtained a copy of the ancient Armenian Bible at Aleppo: with this he retired to a cave for two years, and fasted and prayed. Then Christ revealed himself to him, and told him to go forth and preach repentance, and keep the Sabbath day holy. In obedience to this command he would hold up a serpent, and in the name of the Lord beseech all men to repent. At that time he suffered much persecution; now, these old things have passed away, and all things become new. He is an earnest and devoted preacher of the Gospel in all the towns and villages around, and, from his faithfulness and zeal, is called 'the Apostle to the Gentiles.' I was greatly pleased to find the Bible work of so much interest and importance at Arabkir, on the borders of the ancient Cappadocia.

"The next day we set out upon our journey, escorted on the way by one of the missionaries and several of the native brethren. We passed through a finely cultivated country, abounding in ploughed fields and growing grain, and in six hours came down to the river Euphrates, one of the four rivers that flowed from the garden of Eden. It here runs with a swift current through a rugged gorge, winding among the mountains. Crossing the stream in a primitive scow, with a long rudder that sweeps through the current, we reached the town of Maden, picturesquely situated on the opposite bank. Here a little church of Protestants is gathered through the labors of the American missionaries, and they have a small dépôt for Bibles and Testaments in one corner of their chapel. It was the evening for their social prayer meeting, and they soon all came in to bid us welcome. Then their native preacher conducted the service, reading from the Scriptures and offering prayer. And afterward we addressed them in behalf of the Bible and Mission Cause. They listened with deep interest, and seemed greatly encouraged to feel that Christians in England and America received with them the same pure Bible and Gospel of Salvation.

"It was a peculiar delight to join in the worship of God with these brethren on the banks of the river Euphrates.

"In the morning early we rode over the mountains filled with silver ore, and came to a fine hill country abounding in springs of water, and villages perched upon the hillsides. Thence crossing a fertile plain, and ascending the steep hillside, we reached the fortress-built town of Kharpoot, that overlooks the whole plain and the hundreds of Armenian villages around. The view was most beautiful, as we arrived at the hour of sunset and twilight in the East.

"Kharpoot is one of the more recent missionary stations of the American Board, and is in the centre of a large Armenian population. There are thirty cities within this field, and 366 villages on the plain, containing 100,000 Armenians, 20,000 Koords, and 5,000 Kuzelbash, all accessible to missionary effort. The city is the seat of the pashalic, and a mart of traffic from all parts of Asia Minor. I was glad to find the Scriptures kept publicly for sale, in various languages, near the principal business bazaar: here Turks, Armenians, and Koords from the mountains, come to purchase the Bible. There have been sold, during the last year, twenty-two modern Armenian

Bibles and seventy-one Testaments; five Ancient Armenian and two Turkish Testaments; eight Koordish Gospels; fifty Armenian and five Turkish Psalms; and four English, one Arabic, and one French Testament; making 169 copies of the Scriptures. I visited the two Protestant schools, numbering thirty-three pupils, in which the Scriptures are daily taught. Their system is to commit verses of Scripture, and repeat them on the Sabbath. One little boy, five years old, recited for me nearly the whole of the first chapter of Matthew correctly and well. Also a blind boy seemed quite in advance of the rest in his knowledge of the Scriptures. It was interesting to know that the Bible is likewise taught to the blind in this far off land. Thus the children are instructed to meet and overthrow the corrupt doctrines of the Oriental churches, and defend a pure faith from the Word of God. It is worthy of remark, that the Bible is always made the standard of appeal in every discussion among the common people. In the evening we attended the examination of candidates preparatory to organizing the first Protestant church at Kharpoot. Ten presented themselves for admission. I was much pleased to find all not only sound in doctrine, but also spiritually acquainted with the Scriptures.

"The next day was the Sabbath. In the morning we attended service in the new chapel near

Castle Rock. It was filled with a large and attentive congregation; and after sermon, I briefly addressed them in relation to the Bible Cause, enforcing upon them the duty of circulating the Bible and preaching the Gospel in all the towns and villages around. In the afternoon a still larger audience assembled in the Mission Chapel, to witness the formation of the first evangelical church in the city. The ten candidates then came forward, gave their assent to the confession of faith, and were all baptized and received into membership of the Church of Christ. Among the number was a converted Armenian priest, who became convinced of the truth by studying the Bible, and now received the Gospel anew, in full sincerity and simplicity of heart. Afterward the Rev. Mr. Jones and myself administered to them the communion of the Lord's Supper; and it was a peculiar delight to sit down for the first time with these elect ones around the table of Christ, and partake of the emblems of his death and atonement for the sins of the world. We trust and pray that this may be the beginning of kindling again the pure light of the Gospel of salvation in all this land. In the evening a Turkish effendi, wearing a large white turban, called to see us. He said, 'I have a Testament, and am reading it with much interest; but I cannot understand the doctrine of the Trinity.' We said to him, that we first proved that the Bible was from God; and as this doctrine was revealed in the Bible, we believed its truth; though it might be above the comprehension of our finite minds. He received the remark in silence, and went his way to read again this wondrous Book. The Rev. Mr. Dunmore has also a class of ten young men, to whom he is giving a course of Biblical lectures, and preparing them to go forth and distribute the Bible, and preach the Gospel in all the region round about. We were much interested in the encouraging developments of the missionary work at Kharpoot, and both remarked how entirely it was begun and carried on through the instrumentality of the Bible.

At Diarbekir the native brethren called in to see us, and one of them related the beginning of the good work in the city. A case of Bibles was first sent to Mardin. There they were seized by a rich Catholic merchant, and locked up to keep them from being circulated. The pasha afterwards executed this man in order to obtain his property, and the Bibles were thus set at liberty, and brought to Diarbekir for sale. A Syrian dyer bought one of them, and began to read it aloud at night. This interested one of his workmen, who also obtained a copy, and commenced reading it; then others of the people, till the bishop became alarmed, and ordered all the Bibles to be collected and burned. Still, some were not given up, and the good work went forward, until one of the Syrian bishops himself renounced the errors of his church. He afterwards went to England, and brought out a large number of Bibles, and put them in circulation among his people. Much persecution followed; still the work advanced, in the providence of God, till many were awakened to the truth, and some have remained firm to the end.

"It was most interesting to hear these persecuted ones themselves relate their simple story, and tell what they had suffered for the sake of the Bible and the Gospel of Christ.

"I also called upon the Armenian bishop. He was a venerable old man, with a flowing white beard, and received me with the greatest politeness. I expressed to him the desire of the American Bible Society to furnish every family with the Bible in the modern language which all can understand. He replied, 'It is eyi, chok eyi'—good, very good. 'The bible teaches us the way to heaven. There is one Saviour for English, Americans, and Armenians. Through the blood of Christ we all find salvation, and we are brothers in Christ Jesus.' He says, 'It is a shame if every family who can read does not have the Bible.' As we leave, he presses us warmly by the hand, and remarks, 'In Christ, I hope we may meet in heaven.'

"It is pleasant thus to find that more enlightened views are beginning to prevail among the patriarchs and bishops of the Oriental churches, in reference to the circulation of the Bible and fellowship of the Gospel. On the Sabbath we attended the large Bible class held in the mission chapel. There were 140 present, seated upon their knees in Eastern style. After the lesson, I addressed them in behalf of the Bible Cause. They listened with tears in their eyes, and then crowded around to shake me by the hand and thank me and our Society for sending them the Bible and Gospel to teach them of Christ and the way of eternal salvation; and it was a scene of deep interest, as Syrians, Chaldeans, Greeks, and Armenians, all came forward to express their gratitude in the name, and for the love of Christ.

"In the afternoon, we celebrated with them the communion of the Lord's Supper, and truly sat together in heavenly places in Christ Jesus, calling to mind his sufferings and death upon the cross for our salvation.

"One hundred and sixty copies of the Scriptures have been sold and distributed from this station during the last nine months. They also send out native helpers to sell and distribute the Scriptures in the towns and villages around, and to make tours in the mountains of Koordistan. Thus, through various means, the Word of God is having free course and is glorified in this ancient land.

"At Hassankeifa, the city hewn in rock, I counted seven large mosques, in the finest style of Saracenic architecture, now crumbling to ruins near the city. As I sat among these ruins reading the Bible, one of the Turkish soldiers, who had taken passage with us upon the raft, stepped up to me, and asked if it was the 'Ingil Sheriff' —the holy Gospel. I answered, 'Yes, and I also have one in Turkish, if you wish.' Immediately upon my return he came to me, and begged a Testament; and as I gave it to him, he began at once to read it aloud, that all his companions might hear; and every day since, upon the raft, I have heard him reading his Testament aloud to himself and his fellows with much earnestness. Our earnest prayer is that it may lead him to renounce the religion of the false prophet, and sincerely receive the truth as it is in Jesus.

CHAPTER XX.

HIS JOURNAL.

MR. RIGHTER kept a journal or diary, containing brief notes of the events of each day, during all the time of his second absence from home, until his last illness. Several volumes of such notes were returned to his friends, but they are so brief as not to admit of being transcribed. They were more full on this last journey than they had been before, and it is the source of very deep interest to those who were acquainted with him, and it will be to all into whose hands this volume may fall, that his last records were so full. They show more conclusively than the testimony of others, how truly his heart was devoted to the great work in which he was engaged —how untiring he was in its prosecution, and how cheerfully and even joyfully he arose each day to enter upon its duties and toils. This journal is given entire from the day of his reaching Mosul.

NOVEMBER 8th, 1856.

"A splendid clear morning, and are rejoiced at

the prospect of reaching Mosul in a few hours, and meeting with our excellent Crhistian friends there.

"At noon we came in sight of the minarets and walls of Mosul and Nebly Yonas, the tomb of Jonas covering the ruins of ancient Nineveh, on the opposite side of the river. It is beautiful in the distance, under the clear sunlight of an oriental sky. The shores are clothed with green; the river flows with a broad and majestic current; the walls rise grandly in front, and I greatly enjoy the scene as we float on quietly toward both the ancient and modern city. See several of the native women on the banks of the river, their long black hair flowing down their shoulders in graceful style. The shores are also planted with watermelons that are just gathered for the market.

"The city now stands out fully before us with its walls, battlements, minarets, and towers, in stately oriental style. Sail beside the city walls —count 300 women washing and beating clothes by the river side. Come to anchor near the bridge of boats; are received by a mingled crowd of turbaned natives; a guide directs us through the muddy streets, like Stamboul, towards the house of the American missionaries; meet Mr. Marsh and Dr. Haskell coming to meet us on horseback—insist upon our mounting and riding

—streets, coffee-shops, quite like Eastern cities. Arrive at the mission house—large court with a large tree and singing birds in the centre—cordial welcome; see Mrs. Marsh and Mrs. Lobdue and the children. Ride out upon the plain outside of the city; quite like Egypt in the sky and view, and mild, mellow light. Excellent Arab horses; much enjoy the ride, also a fine walk on the housetop and view over the city. Have a delightful social prayer-meeting with the missionaries in the evening.

SABBATH, 9th.

"Am awaked by the cheerful singing of birds in the court. This morning see *Kos-ma-chiel* who was formerly a Catholic Nestorian priest, and was in Rome five months where he became a Protestant.

"Attend the Bible class in the chapel; fifty or sixty were present, seated on their knees in Eastern style—venerable, fine-looking men wearing large round turbans. I address them in behalf of the Bible cause, visit to Egypt, the Crimea, and the Kuzelbash. They listen with much interest, and then come forward to shake me by the hand and thank the American Bible Society for sending them the Bible and gospel of salvation. It was an impressive scene as these Syrians, descendants of the old Assyrians, in sight of the ruins of ancient Nineveh, thus expressed their gratitude for receiving the word of God at our hands.

"I was much pleased with the neat chapel and intelligent congregation. In the evening have a meeting for organizing a branch of the Evangelical Alliance. After hearing of the Turkey branch of the Alliance, and discussing the matter with much interest, they unanimously and cordially expressed their desire to form a branch, and thus be linked with Christians in all parts of the East and the world. It was a meeting of much interest. They cheerfully came forward and signed their names in Arabic to our rules and regulations—fourteen members, all who could write.

"The women wear a black mask upon their heads, which, when it is drawn, entirely conceals their face.

MONDAY, 10th.

"Another very delightful morning. Ride on horseback to the Pasha's palace. Very pleasant reception by the Pasha in his audience room, overlooking the Tigris. Hamdi Pasha, a fine-looking gentlemen of the modern school, heartily shook hands with us, and bid us welcome. He had not often the honor of a visit from English and Americans; entertains us with chebouks, preserves, and coffee in oriental style. He hoped that a friendly intercourse with each other would increase; it would be to our mutual benefit. He remarked that now Mussulmans and Christians and Jews were becoming brothers. My friend said we have one Father. 'Yes,' he replied, 'Allah was Lord of all the earth; not only the God of the mountains but also of the plains.' I remarked his views were the same as the Sultan's, as declared in the Hatti humayoun. 'Yes,' said he, 'the Firman was read in Arabic and Turkish in the grand court of the palace to all the people, and it would be his object to have it fully carried out.' He greatly rejoiced in it. In comparing the present with the past great advance was made. The meaning of the word Koort was originally wolf, and it was now *dog*, and he hoped they would soon make it *sheep*. He pressed us to take a guard of his soldiers that we might pass with honor through the country. He rose as we left, and took leave of us with friendly salutations, 'salam safa guelding Khosh guelding,' —welcome, much welcome. He would do us the favor of returning our visit. Then we call upon the Deftudar Kyiah, who received us in a similar cordial manner, entertained us in the same style, and expressed the same enlightened views in regard to English and Americans. The Pasha had been six years from Stamboul, and his secretary the same. We were greatly delighted with our visit thus far, in the interior. Call to visit the Bible dépôt, at the large new Khan of the English consulate, near the two principal gates of the city. Bibles in Arabic, Syriac, ancient and modern—a very public place and well known in the city. Copies of the Scriptures sold during the last year; 217 books, of which 34 were Scriptures and parts of Scriptures. Call upon Mrs. Rassam, wife of the English Consul; fine house, large court, garden in the centre, slabs from Nineveh in the pavement, and beautiful sedab or alabaster underground apartment below. Then visit the dispensary and see Dr. Haskel in his labors of love, prescribing for the crowd of patients of all classes, Moslems, Christians, and Jews, women, men, and children, who daily come to him. They average forty or fifty each day. The system is first to preach the gospel to them, and then give them medicine for their diseases—Arabs from the desert, Koords from the mountains, Moslems and Christians from the city.

"Mosul has a population of 45,000; Moslems 36,000; Christians 7,500; 1,500 Jews; about two-fifths ancient Syrians or Jacobites; two-fifths Chaldeans or Papal Nestorians; one-fifth Papal Syrians; 180 enrolled in the Protestant community; fifteen church members; attendance at service (average fifty-five); language used entirely Arabic. A Bible class of twenty or thirty; two boys' schools numbering sixty pupils; three natives are employed in going from house to house to teach the men and women to read the Bible in the families; have three preachers—Jeremiah Shemmas, deacon, Kos Machiel (formerly a Papal Nestorian priest), Behnan, from the seminary of Aleih; three teachers; have three out stations at Jezerch, a village near *Nahauan*, where the Nestorian priest and his people are Protestant, numbering 100. He teaches the people to read the Bible.

"Spend a very pleasant evening with the French Consul, his adopted daughter, and Mrs. R——— quite like an American evening party—save the variety of languages spoken, English, French, Italian, Turkish, Arabic, and Greek.

TUESDAY, 11th.

"After the rain it is mild and genial this morning. This morning the Pasha, according to appointment, calls to visit us, accompanied by his defterdar and an interpreter. He brings his own chibouque and fingaw, says that one American friend has brought him two others, and he is now rich. I tell him that I hope the ships sailing from America on the chart before him will bring him many more. He smiles approbation and says that he felt in his heart that there was something good near him, but he was not aware of so great an affair so close beside him. He remarked that some physicians give a medicine to cure one disease, others give a medicine to heal and renew the system. So a good government should seek for gradual reforms. I remarked, his views entirely coincided with the ideas of the Sultan, in the Hatti Sheriff. I told him that we were so much pleased with his liberal sentiments we would be happy to present him with a copy of the Bible that he might learn what we in England and America believed. He expressed his thanks, and said it would be valuable in two particulars; it would always remind him of his true friend; and it would be good for instruction, as being the book of God. He was exceeding affable and gracious —remarkably intelligent, and ready at repartee— a good specimen of an active-minded Turk.

"The conversation continued for a half hour more, and he took his leave in Oriental style. His Secretary, when we inquired with regard to fine Arab horses, said, the son of the Pasha had one, and his own were the best in Mosul.

"He invited us, in the court, to see his, a noble animal of full blood and breeding, whereupon he gave us the favor of riding her to visit ancient Nineveh, and he himself volunteered to accompany us, as he was acquainted with Mr. Layard and his excavations. We rode out in grand style, six in our party—crossing the floating bridge over the Tigris, we galloped across the plain and along the line of the ancient walls which are distinctly traceable to the mound of one of the palace gateways. Here we dismounted and descended into the trenches under ground. I was amused to find here one of the largest human-headed winged bulls standing in its original site at the entrance of a temple. And near by was a full length figure of a priest, holding in his hand the sacred cone in offering sacrifice to the deity before him. Both were cut in solid stone, and were of huge dimensions. On the opposite side stands another of similar size to guard the porch of the temple. Then we walk in and examine the sides of the room. Slabs are inlaid, exceedingly interesting. We then walked to the exterior top of the mound and traced the line of the ancient walls of the city seven miles in circuit. Yonder is the buried ruin of the temple palace of Koyunjuk, and beyond the mound and tomb of the prophet Jonas, over which a splendid Moslem mosque is now erected, and a little Moslem village built around it, which has not been excavated underneath. Descending, we mounted our horses and galloped within the city walls. It is now a ploughed field, as the common houses were of sun-dried bricks, all was consumed, and crumbled to ruins. Then we came to the palace mound of Koyunjuk. This has been extensively excavated, and here the most valuable articles were found. We descend into the trenches, and come to the grand hall of the palace; here were splendid column pedestals, a finely wrought slab of pavement, and slabs and remains of ancient art and skill extending far. Then we walked over the mound, saw various shafts and trenches, and at length descended and came to another temple—four huge bulls at the gateway; one of them at the side covered with cuneiform inscriptions, and in the hall slabs of battle and triumphal scenes, attacking a fortified town, casting up a mound, battering-rams, hurling stones; and another represents ancient *Tyre*, palm trees, fish, a man carrying a banner, etc.; another represents a hill country, etc. Also we see the instruments of music played, cymbals, tamborine and harp. We could have wandered a whole day here. Next we rode to the village of Nebly Yonas. Ascend to the Mosque. The dignified old Moslem admits us to the Mosque. It is elegantly built in a dome style, and richly carpeted within. We walk to the tomb of the prophet underneath a small dome; here we look through a grated window, strung with many-colored pilgrim rags. Then we ask to enter within to the tomb itself. After some little hesitation, they light their long sacred candles, and unlock the heavy door. Solemnly they advance praying to Allah, and bow on the knee as we come in front of the tomb. It is richly carpeted with Persian carpet. We descended six steps and walked around the tomb. It is covered with rich green silk, and above a splendid gold cloth, given by the Pasha of Busru. Then we came into the court of the Mosque, and ascend the beautiful glazed brick minaret. The view was magnificent, in the clear sunlight, of the ancient city; its walls and gateway, towers, temples—the winding Tigris stretching afar—the gardens opposite—the flocks and Arab tents, and the mountains of the Kurdistan rising majestically behind, a scene of vivid interest I shall never forget. Then we descend, mount our horses and gallop over the plain and across the river to Mosul.

"Make a pleasant evening call upon the French consul, at his house, a good specimen of French politeness. Learn the news, political crisis coming on, and the prospect of another Congress at Paris.

"Have a beautiful moonlight view from the housetop of Mr. Marsh. The pure and mellow light shedding over the scene. Venus just setting in the west and Jupiter shining clear in the sky, like the views of moonlight scene from the housetop in Jerusalem. Talk late in the evening with Mr. Marsh on various interesting matters.

WEDNESDAY, 12.

Call first upon our friend, the Pasha's defterdar, a Christian. He receives us in a most cordial manner, entertained us with narghile, sherbet, coffee, and preserves, etc., in oriental style. Then he introduced his wife, a fine-looking, tall woman, splendidly dressed in figured silk skirt, gold embroidered vest, golden necklace, and golden head-dress, inwrought with precious stones. Express our pleasure at seeing a native Christian lady in a social call at Mosul, far in the East.

We call our wives in America our better half, but Moslems degrade them. Thinks a Moslem would be killed by the people for becoming Christian, but not by the government. The authorities would execute the murderers. He himself wears the decoration of Mejedie, the first ever conferred on a Christian. Three papal Syrian priests were present, who had been to Rome, and assisted in the entertainment. They spoke Italian.

Then the son of the Pasha sent his Arab horse for us to see. A large iron grey, splendidly formed, strong, a noble creature from the Shummur tribe.

Afterward call upon the Syrian Archbishop, a venerable man with a long, flowing beard, intelligent and affable; received us with great courtesy; says he makes the Bible the only rule of faith, preaches from the word of God alone; read us one of his sermons in Syriac, beautifully written, on the new heart—except a man be born again he cannot enter the kingdom of heaven. If a sinner came to inquire the way of salvation he would show him the word of God. Thy word is a light to my feet, etc. He seems thoroughly evangelical in his views, and wishes to publish them in a book. The word of God is like a net to catch sinners, and pull them out of their sins. Tell him we hope he will become the Luther of the Syrian church—one-third of his people sympathise with him in these spiritual views—we must walk by the word of God. The heavens and the earth pass away, but the word of the Lord endureth for ever. He is a thorough Bible man. Tell him I am glad to hear that he founds his faith on the word of God. I ask him if he wishes his people to have the Bible in their families, to read and learn the way of salvation. He would rejoice in it, and he himself will distribute and sell the Bible to all who desire it. He wishes Syriac, Arac, and Arabic in Syriac character (gershuni). He prayed that himself and the missionaries may all be one in their *spiritual* labors for their people, and that the time might soon come when they would preach in each other's pulpits, and partake of the communion of Christ together around the table of Christ. Immediately after he wishes the Dr. Haskell to prescribe for him.

Then call to visit the house of Dr. Grant, now occupied by a Syrian family. The two women are at home, one of them knew Dr. Grant. He had healed her of a disease. The Lord have mercy on him. The other was very beautiful and dressed in a profusion of gold ornaments, nose jewels, and bracelets and anklets. They were exceeding polite. Saw the room in which Dr. G. died, looking out on the Tigris, with stained glass windows above. (May our last end be like his. See the man who saw his death scene.)

Here is a beautiful view from the house-top over the city. Mr. Laurie and Layard afterward lived here.

Then call upon Mrs. Russan, visit the Protestant school of twenty-seven Syrian boys. Answer Bible questions and one of them read from the Testament very fluently—nine years old. Mrs. Marsh and Mrs. Lobdell have a meeting one day in a week, in which the Scriptures are read and explained to them and prayer is offered. The average number of twenty attend, also a Bible class on Sunday of fourteen members. There is also a Bible society organized among the church members, appropriating a fund of a hundred piastres a year for distributing the Scriptures to the poor.

"Ride outside the city walls at the hour of sunset to see the (American) missionary burial-ground. Visit the graves of Drs. Grant and Lobdell, Mr. Laurie, Mrs. Mitchell and Williams, Mr. Hinsdale, and the children of the missionaries who have died here. It is beautifully situated on a slightly elevated ground, one mile from the city, in sight of the gardens, river Tigris, Jonah's tomb, and the snow-crowned mountains of Kurdistan in the distance. Blessed are the dead that die in the Lord.

"THURSDAY, 13.

"Have a very pleasant call from the Syrian *Archbishop Behnan* (*Maphrian, see Mosheim*). He wishes our assistance to secure justice to one of his Syrian people. We tell him there is an Evangelical Alliance at Constantinople, formed for this very object, and we would be glad to have him a member. Read to him the list of officers, the Dutch ambassador, Bishop Gobat, Mr. Nicolayson. He replies, it is very good, and he will think of it. He says the Papists have much opposed his work. I answer they have also opposed us in circulating the Bible. No Papists are members of this Alliance, only those who receive the Bible as their rule of faith. He says woe to him that standeth alone, see Jeremiah. We are one if we are born of the Holy Spirit, one in Christ

Jesus. Tell him our desire to introduce the Bible into his school. He will be very thankful to have them. A very excellent, evangelical, intelligent, and interesting Archbishop of the (Oriental) Syrian Church.

"In the evening have a meeting of the teachers of schools, and the boys who go from house to house to teach the natives, both men and women, to read, and instruct them in the Scriptures. A chapter is read in the Bible, questions asked, and an appropriate prayer offered by one of the teachers, and then we both addressed them on the importance of their work.

"FRIDAY, 14.

"In the morning the kiljah of the Pasha calls. He is a very affable and courteous man. Tell him that my name originally signified *Richter*, Judge, cadi in Turkish, and English it is Righter (Daha Dogree). He says, we love you yourself and still more for your name. I ask him for his name, and its signification. *Ismidt* (Glory). Tell him I am happy to see that the glory of his name has not departed. His ancestors won glory, and mine justice and right. He was a fine specimen of a complimentary Turkish courtier.

"Engages to send us a bourneti and cavasses for our journey in the mountains.

"Then we arrange with our katergio. After

we had finished our arrangements, to our great surprise, one of these rough *muleteers* burst forth with a volley of English words that perfectly amazed us.

" Ride out with the ladies just at sunset and golden twilight. The evening star, the purity of the western horizon bounding the desert afar, and Jupiter brilliant in the blue sky, formed a scene of picturesque beauty I shall never forget, more like heaven than a scene of earth.

"In the evening the Syrian Archbishop sends us his servant to bear his Christian salutation and a sermon on the Word of God, saying that his mind has been spiritually stirred up by our visit, and he is more desirous than ever to be zealously engaged in the cause of Christ. The discourse was translated to us, and was an excellent scriptural sermon. We wrote his Grace an epistle in behalf of evangelical Christians in England and America, and requesting a copy of the sermon for publication; also the Archbishop's views on the 'all important doctrine of justification by faith.'

"SATURDAY, 15.

" In the morning we ride across the floating-bridge on the Tigris, and then gallop on and around the walls of Nineveh. We set out at the tomb of Jonah, and riding upon the top of the wall, we came to the angle of the wall that commands a view down the river, at the south, toward Nimroud. Then we rode on, passing by the gateways at the sides, and came to an angle on the east that looks toward the snow crowned mountains of Kurdistan. The walls are still 20 feet high, and steep, wide enough for a horse to gallop on the top, though built of sun-dried bricks, and subject for two thousand years to the action of the elements and the hand of man; at the bottom they are at least forty feet wide. Passing northward, we observed at the side traces of an outer wall, forming a wide trench between. We also distinctly marked gateways at intervals upon this side. In the centre a river flows directly through the city. On the northern angle there is a large mound, and also a palace gateway at the west, where huge winged bulls were found and sculptured slabs. The view from this point is beautiful, up the winding river toward the distant mountains, as well to Mosul and the desert stretching far beyond. Then we rode to Koyunjuk, filled with excavations, and returned to our point of starting Nebly Yonas.

"The river originally, in all probability, flowed near the walls, and the gates were more frequent on the river side. The walls are now ploughed and sowed with grain, and Nineveh is also a ploughed field, and used as a place for spreading nets to catch birds. It was most interesting thus to circumvent the walls, and behold the complete desolation of this ancient city under the judgment of God. We occupied an hour and a half in our ride of eight miles. The air was pure and bracing, and much we enjoyed the scene.

"Returning we held a conference, by special appointment, with the Syrian Archbishop, at the house of the English Consul. He expresses a willingness to join the Evangelical Alliance. He also desires to leave the errors of his church, and unite with the Church of England, if he can meet with sympathy and support. Or he will give up all, if need be, and hire a chapel and there preach only the Gospel and the Word of God. He seems to be very sincere, and we trust and pray that the Lord will abundantly strengthen him to do his will. It was a deeply interesting interview. In the evening made our final arrangements for departure on Monday.

"SUNDAY, 16.

"Attend Arabic service early in the morning, at the hour of sunrise. Mr. Marsh preaches on the third commandment. It is a pleasant hour to meet together for the worship of God. At eleven Mr. Jones gives us a sermon in English, 'My heart is fixed,' etc. Then we call upon the Archbishop and find him quite ill. He is unable to enter farther into the subject of the Evangelical

Alliance; wishes it to be carried forward in writing through Mrs. Russam. He seems very sincere, and entirely disposed to take the Bible alone for his rule of faith, and the Gospel for his hope of salvation. I tell him our prayer will be that the Holy Spirit may guide him in the way of all truth, and that we may meet in heaven at last. In the afternoon we have the communion service when Mr. Jones and I address them. It was a most interesting and solemn occasion. In the evening the native brethren meet at the house of Mr. Marsh, and he questions them upon the preaching of the day, and conducts prayers in Arabic. Again they thank us for coming from England and America to visit them in the name of Christ.

"MONDAY, 17.

"The Pasha sends his salaams, and regrets that himself, defterdar, and suite could not escort us out of the city, as the post had just arrived.

"At noon the katugi and his animals come, and the cavasses, ready for our departure. We set out in due time, a highly respectable party in numbers and appearance. Dr. Haskell joins us. The native brethren on foot accompany us, and our friend Houaza Yohanna, wearing his decoration, and mounted on his fine Arab mare, beautifully caparisoned, escorts us across the river and some distance beyond. A cavass from the Pacha, and four zabtiers as a guard, accompany us. My Arab steed, Emir, is in full spirit, and we gallop on beautifully over the plain. The snow-covered mountains are in front, tinged with purple light, and the whole western sky is flooded with golden light. The air is mild and genial, and much I enjoy it. Mr. Marsh also joins us for the first night. Just at twilight we reach Tell Kef, a large town of 2,000 inhabitants, all Papal Nestorians or Chaldeans (Mussulmans and Christians). We are most comfortable, in a large, well-finished room, with a good fire, and an excellent dinner.

"TUESDAY, 18.

"Have a comfortable night. The view from the country is beautiful. Gallop on over the plain past two Syrian villages, and in four hours arrive at El Rosh. It is beautifully situated just at the base of the mountain range.

"The fig, pomegranate, and evergreen trees are growing beside the fountain and stream that flows through. This was the birthplace of the Prophet Nahum and the Elkoshite. He has often ploughed these fields and looked upon these scenes. We are very cordially received by the Kahyah Yusef, a Chaldean. He says that English, Americans, Chaldeans, are all one in Christ. Christ is our Master and Head.

"He speaks in the highest terms of Dr. Grant;

says he was an excellent man, and has been in the village and in this very room.

"After lunch, visited the tomb of the Prophet in a small church underneath the mountain. It is a small round tomb, covered with Persian cloth. We then ride on to a Yesidi village. It is very neat and comfortable. A woman runs down the hill to the doctor, and begs for medicine. Then we ride over a stony road past several Yesidi villages. There were two large mounds on the plain. Oleanders are growing by the brooks. We start up gazelles near the mountain. They are beautiful creatures as they nimbly leap among the rocks. Just after sunset we reach the Yesidi village of Baadri. It is situated in a little valley with a stream flowing through, and planted with green trees. It is very neat and thrifty in appearance.

"Hassein Bey, to whom we have letters of introduction, receives in very gracious manner, shaking us cordially by the hand, and bidding us welcome. He is a young man of amiable and agreeable address. The village contains a population of 500.

"WEDNESDAY, 19.

"Have a very comfortable night. In the morning our chief calls upon us and takes a cup of coffee. Then we call the Moolah, and present him with a copy of the Bible. He receives it very reverentially, and his priest began to read both in the Old and New Testament of the Creation and Christ. Tell him we love this much in England and America. That we have much money, but we value this above all. That comes from the earth, this from God. He says he will read in it every day, and also to the people of his village. Tell him this speaks of Jesus Christ, who came from heaven, and through faith in Christ we hope to reach heaven. It was a most interesting scene.

"Then the Bey walks with us to a hill that overlooks the village. Here is the ruin of his father's Palace, destroyed by Raroudoz Bey. The view is beautiful. Over the plain are sixty villages of Yesidis. As we come down we enter a native house. It is very neat and well constructed. Now we mount our horses, and the chief, with twenty horsemen, his son, Hassan, accompanies us. As the word is given, and the horses gallop on, the spears glitter in the sunlight, the music sounds. It is a gay and brilliant scene. Two are richly dressed in gold-embroidered red suits. The sheik is dressed in a light brown suit, neatly embroidered, and mounted on a fine black horse of Yesidi breed. Hassan, his son, is dressed in scarlet, and though only seven, rides a grey mare beautifully. It is a beautiful view over the hill as they gallop around in circles, and then close around their chief. In one hour we come to a white pointed tomb; they dismount and kiss a flat stone in front, repeating a short prayer, and then ride on, singing as they go their native song. In another hour we come to a small ravine, through which a clear stream flows, and it is planted with oleanders and green trees.

We now move on in single file for a half hour —come in sight of the white spires of Sheik Avi. Descending to a small valley they all dismount and pull off their shoes, and walk up to their sacred shrine. The chief folds his hands in front and walks barefoot in solemn style. It is a beautifully shaded place—green olive trees, oaks, with autumn tint and various shades; the brook rustles through, and the birds are singing in the branches. I walk beside the Bey, and we enter the outer court of their temple. He and his men all walk around and kiss the sacred stones, and then we sit down under the shade of a large overspreading vine to lunch. A stream of clear water is running through, and birds are singing beautifully. The blacksnake and hatchet are upon the wall outside. It is one of the most interesting visits I have ever made, and all are so amiable and courteous I cannot realize that we are in the midst of the hated devil worshippers. Then the door of their temple was opened, and we entered. A large fountain of water is in one side, and at the other two tombs with curtains drawn before them. One is said to contain the devil's head. Lamps are kept continually burning before them. I then presented the sheik with a copy of the Bible, in Arabic, to be kept in their temple and read at their festivals, and whenever any one came who wished to read it. We then gave our cards to Hassein Bey and gave him our parting salutations. He was exceedingly gracious and gentle to the last. I was greatly pleased with him, and trust our visit will do good to the Yesidis. He gives us two horsemen, with spears, and one footman, as a guard and guide. The valley is exceedingly romantic and beautiful, planted with the fig, the olive, and the oak, and resounding with the notes of singing birds. We now pursue a hilly winding road—past black Koordish tents and small villages, and then come to a wild ravine with a stream dashing over the rocks and the mountain rising steep on either side —a scene of great wildness and beauty. The road is rough and steep. In two hours more climbing up the mountain side, we came to the village of *Bebosi*, all Chaldeans or Catholic Nestorians.

"THURSDAY, 20.

"Sleep well in a warm native house. The views

at sunrise from the housetop in the midst of the mountains are beautiful. The reddening and the rosy light. The village is partly in ruins. Ride on through a rocky wooded glen, where figs and olives grow in the valley, and oaks cover the mountain side, and rest at an angle of the road in a shady spot refreshed by the cooling breeze. In a half hour we come to a point that commands a view over a fertile valley with villages at the side, and a wild deep ravine winding through the mountain. Descending thence, we lunched under a wide-spreading oak, with this scene stretching before us. We rode on over steep, rough, rocky mountains, and in four hours arrived at the village of Spindura, upon a sloping hillside. There was much excitement upon our arrival; nearly the whole village turned out on the housetops to witness the important event. The population is three hundred and fifty, entirely Moslems.

"FRIDAY, 21.

"The patients come round in the morning to show their diseases and receive their medicines with much gratitude. We ride three hours over a very rugged mountain, and lunch in a quiet little valley by a clear stream flowing down the mountain. Then three hours more over a rough road intersected by ravines and come in sight of Amadia, perched high upon the rocks. We toiled up the steep hillside late in the evening, and find the large gate shut. We rap at the gate, and they hail us from the wall to inquire who we are, and where we came from. Our cavass replies, that he is Achmet Effendi, the Pasha's man, and a distinguished party had arrived. They, however, had heard our guns of salute fired and suspect us of being a party of robber Koords, fifteen in number. The cavass says we have come from the Pasha, and have a firman from the Sultan. The capugi replies, I do not know who you are; and thus we are kept waiting an hour in the cold and dark. At length the Moodir and several of his principal men came with lanterns, and the gates were opened with great carefulness and display. How great was our delight when our good friend Shemmas Jeremiah of Mosul, embraced us, and bid us welcome. The Moodir also extended both hands, and bid us welcome. He had walked down from his palace to receive us, and his suite accompanied us to the Serai. There his largest room fitted for our reception, and a warm fire made us most comfortable. Immediately he ordered an oriental dinner of six or eight courses, rice, chickens, mutton, cakes, preserves, etc., and closes up with chibouk, coffee, and sherbet. He gives us also a warm cloak of fur. Our room is hung round with various arms, swords, pistols, guns, for impressive effect.

"SATURDAY, 22.

"A beautiful, clear morning of pure air. The Dr. has many patients, the Moodir's wife's sister, the Usbashi (Major), etc. One of them says he is not sick, but wishes to get fat like the Moodir. Go to see three full length sculptures of kings, cut in the rock outside the wall, very ancient, now much broken and defaced. Then we make a call upon the Usbashi (Major), at the barracks. The Pasha's commissioners are there. They rise as we approach, and receive us upon carpets and cushions in the open air. The sky is pure, and the air delightful, and the view of the mountain ranges, the valley and villages, and the whole panorama around is magnificent.

"The priest from *Deirra*, a Nestorian village, one hour distant, calls to see us, population fifty. Six can read, have the Bible in the church, and have Testaments in the village; wishes all to have the Testament. He preaches when they have the sacrament, twenty or thirty times a year. He preaches repentance, has a congregation of forty; has prayers every day, morning and evening, and two services on Sunday. Just now a band of the Moodir's Koordish soldiers return from one of the mountain districts, armed with guns and swords, on foot and on horseback, with the music of drums, in great style. They had been out to gather taxes from the villages around.

Then we call upon the Moodir and Commissioners, in his reception room, and have an audience with them; very pleasant. In the evening Shemmas Jeremiah relates his history and experience. He was a Catholic Nestorian or Chaldean monk, in a convent near Elkosh. He was directed to the 1*st of Timothy*, 4th chapter, first three verses. He reflected upon this, went to the missionaries at Mosul, Dr. Perkins and Mr. Stocking, from Oroomeah. He went with them and taught in their schools, and there embraced the truth. Amadich has a population of 2,500, of whom 2000 are Moslems, 350 Syrians, 100 Nestorians, and 50 Jews; formerly it contained 14,000, and was the residence of the Sultan.

"SUNDAY, 23.

"This morning the brother of Osman Bey, Abuzed Bey, the Koordish chief, calls to see us. We then receive a call from the Moodir. He offers us his horse to ride out and visit the Nestorians in Dare. We descend the steep hill-side without the walls. On the right is a beautiful valley, planted with trees and gardens. In a few minutes the priest, on horseback, and a number of his people come out to meet us, and escort us to their village. We climb a steep hill and then come down to Dare, a beautiful little village under the high mountain rock. A pure spring of water gushes out and flows down the valley. Trees and fertile gardens with nuts, pomegranates, figs, and grapes are in front. We visit the church, a large stone building with three arched rooms. They have cotton, nuts, onions, and various fruit offerings given to support the church. We send to call the people, and they assemble, old men, women, and children, priest and deacon, thirty in number, when we all preach to them the Gospel of salvation, through faith in Christ. They listen with much interest and reverence, and respond frequently to the word of everlasting life.

"Then we sit out with them in the open air, they gather around on their knees in a circle, and say they will put a chain upon us to keep us long with them. The summer retreat of the Mosul missionaries is here.

"There are no pictures in the church but a small cross, which they say they kiss from love to Christ. Then they bring us a lunch of pomegranates, honey, nuts, eggs, and bread, which we eat in the shade, and much enjoy it together. After which we talk further of Christ and his cross, etc., and then ride down to Komani, past fields of rice, cotton, wheat, tobacco, and gardens of various fruit trees. Komani has a new, neat church, and contains a population of 300, all Nestorians. The people are delighted to see us, and salute us with much respect and reverence. We called them into the church, and spoke to them of their sins, Christ, repentance, and eternal salvation. They listened with intense interest and frequently responded, and seemed greatly to enjoy the truth. They desire much to have an American missionary to come and live among them, to teach them the Bible and to preach to them the Gospel of salvation. Eight in the village can read and they have no Bible. It was a Sabbath of great interest among the mountain Nestorians. They are a simple-hearted, pure-minded people, and entirely ready to receive the Gospel.

"We also visited the house where Dr. Grant lived in Amadia. There he spent some time in the midst of his labors of love and mercy to this people. The owner of the house, a venerable old man, lived with him. He says since the days of Adam in the flesh, there was never such a man. He prayed much, read his Bible, and preached the Gospel to all. The Holy Ghost was with him in all that he said and did.

"MONDAY, 24.

"This morning the Moodir calls upon us, and the Usbashi, or commander of the fortress, and a number of patients came for medicine. Then a Moslem sheik and the Usbashi, or Major of the troops. Afterward the Commissioners of the Pasha came in to smoke a chibouk and take coffee with us, and then Osman Bey, the Koordish chief, a very bold, fearless man in appearance, and having much of the fierce spirit of his native mountains. See also the woman, a widow and her daughter, who had been stripped of all her possessions by a plundering Koordish chief, and listen to her tale of oppression and wrong. Saw also one Jew, a probable descendant of the ten captive tribes. He says there are 500 Jews in Amadia. They have been waiting 1800 years for (Christ) the Messiah, and he has not come yet.

"TUESDAY, 25.

"Aalam Effendi Moodir, of Amadieh, a very kind, hospitable man.

"A cold foggy rainy morning. The snow is on the mountains. The Moodir, mounted on his Arab horse, with a band of his attendants and a band of music, escorted us out of the city, and then he gives us his salaams in parting. We ride over to the Nestorian village of Bibudi. The villagers all gather on the housetops to welcome us; they are exceedingly friendly. It is a wedding day, and they are all dressed in their gay clothing. The church is a very neat stone building with a low door. They all come around, priests, deacons, men, women, and children, and we preach the Gospel to them; tell them to believe the Bible, trust in God, have faith in Christ, and pray for the Holy Spirit to dwell in their hearts, and guide them to everlasting life. They heartily respond, and greatly desire a missionary to live among them, and teach them the way of eternal salvation; they wished that we should stay with them. The village is beautifully situated under the mountain range, and overlooking the valley. We then pursue our way. The fog rests on the mountain, and clears from the landscape before us. The sun shines out underneath the clouds upon the white waterfalls and snow-capped peaks, like a scene of resplendent glory, more beautiful in its effect than any I have ever before seen. Pass through two Chaldean Catholic Nestorian villages, and arrive at evening at Daoudich. The Moodir Achmed Effendi, a very pleasant gentleman, receives us with much hospitality and gives us a cordial reception in his palace castle. The landscape to day was most beautiful. The fields are cultivated with grain, rice, and olive trees. The mountain ranges rise on either hand, and the valley stretches before us in picturesque and varied beauty.

"Daoudich contains a population of eighty Catholic Nestorians. A small Nestorian village is about one hour distant. We have a very animated conversation in the evening with the Moodir, on the subject of religious liberty. He says there is the same God over Moslems, Christians, Jews, and Yesidees, and all should be brothers.

"WEDNESDAY, 26.

"A fine view from the castle fort, of the rugged snow-crowned mountains and beautiful fertile valley around. The Moodir, with his attendants on horseback, accompanies us a short distance on the way. We ride on three hours over a hilly country well cultivated, growing grain and grapes. Guards receive us on the road in military style. Then we come to the village of Baroski; 300, all Mussulmans, very neat. We lunch in a comfortable place. Nice dried grapes are brought to us.

"We take a guard of five men, and travel over a similarly cultivated country, and arrive in two hours at the village of Nereshko for the night. There are sixty inhabitants, all Moslems; the women go unveiled. Our room is filled with wheat, rice, and barley, in sacks piled to the roof. The situation is elevated and beautiful. Fevers seem to prevail in all this region, resulting principally from irrigating the rice and tobacco fields.

"THURSDAY, 27.

"We ride over a hilly country planted with wheat, grain, and cotton, and in two and a half hours come to the Koordish village of Tel Akro, about fifty inhabitants, situated under the hillside. Then we pass across a branch of the Kabour, and beside the large river itself, flowing with a rapid current. The strong castle of a robber chief rises alone on the rugged mountains of Kala. We lunch in a rocky glen beside a little stream of pure water.

"Then we continue on our way and come to a Koordish encampment, cochers, robbers, in a little valley of black tents. Afterward we ride along the river Kabour, the ancient Chebar, and in two hours come in sight of Zakho. A large tower castle rises in front, and two bridges across the river; the first called Del Ali, pretty woman, so called because a Koordish chief saw her there. We arrive at 4 P.M. at Zakho, and are received very respectfully at first by the Moodir, but a Catholic insists upon having us put in a shabby room. We send for the Moodir, and assert our rights with the Sultan's firman, and he then gives us the first place and good attention. The Moodir is Shemdin Agha, a fine-looking Koord with a black beard. Zakho has a population 2,000; 1,500 Jews, 500 Moslems, 40 Christians.

"The Moodir very politely brings grapes, figs, pomegranates, etc., for our entertainment, and we spend a very pleasant evening, smoking chibouks and drinking coffee sociably together.

"Friday, 28.

"We are now in the Pashalic of Diarbekir. After breakfast the Moodir calls and brings his little son, a fine boy, with his sword girt on. Then go to visit the Jews; find them in the synagogue at their prayers; see the Rabbi, a venerable old man with a white beard; have been here 200 years; show me their Hebrew books, and a copy of the law rolled up like a scroll. They gather around me with much interest; are pleased to know that I have been to Jerusalem; they come from all lands. A very interesting visit. The Moodir mounted on a fine Arab mare, with his guard of honor, escorts us on the way. We cross the bridge of Del Ali, and one hour and a half along the plain, come to the village of Durnoc, now Moslem, formerly Christian. There is here a deserted church now used as a stable. Now we ford the deep river, and ride over the plain one hour, and lunch beside a running brook. We gallop on over the plain, see forty or fifty gazelles, and large birds like ostriches. Here the great battle between Darius and Alexander was fought. In two hours we arrive at the village of Narhawur. 50 population, 25 Protestants and 25 Catholics. Stop at the house of Shemmas Paulo, Deacon Paul, a Protestant, who receives us with much rejoicing. The priest, a Protestant, calls in to visit us, and many of the villagers gather around. He is in the employ of the missionaries, and teaches school in his own house; is a pleasant-looking man with a black beard.

"The situation of the village is beautiful, on a little mound, near a stream of water, overlooking the plain. The sunset scene is lovely from the house-top, the deep, golden light in the west, and the rosy tint resting on the snow-capped mountains, and the whole landscape stretching before me of unusual beauty. The river Kabour flows through, and here doubtless the Prophet Ezekiel saw his sublime visions of Jehovah most high. In the evening fifteen or sixteen of the Nestorians gather in the room of the Kahyah, seated on their knees in a circle, and we speak to them of Christ and the Gospel of salvation. They listen with deep attention. They then tell us of the oppression of the Moslems. There are twenty-two men, and they pay one-tenth of their grain, 1332 piastres tax, and soldiers are quartered upon them, from two to twenty every night without pay, and as it is on the high road, it is a serious grievance. Every forty-four Christians must pay 5000 piastres for one soldier.

"SATURDAY, 29.

"Sleep in the same room with our horses, three apartments, harem, male sleeping-room, and stable. The sunrise view from the house-top is magnificent, over the eastern mountains. Yonder comes the powerful king of day rejoicing in the East. What golden glory gilds his chariot wheels, shedding over the snow-crowned mountain tops. We ride on two hours over the plain, have another gazelle chase, and then we come in sight of the Tigris again. It comes flowing down with a whirling, eddying current. We ride two hours beside the river, and lunch in view of the blue mountains, stretching far in the distance. Soon we come upon an eminence near the Tigris, to the castle and minarets of Jesireh, and then in two hours along the river-side, we arrive at Mansoira, a Nestorian village of 300 population. It commands a fine view of the river, the mountains, and the plain around. The Kahyah comes out on foot to receive us, and politely kisses our hand. He quarters us in a spacious native house, with two large rooms, and a stable attached, separated by a hall. Here we expatiate in grand style, much entertained by the habits of the natives, baking in a round oven; a young girl of sixteen pounding bulgoar in a stone mortar, with a huge mallet. They gather in our room in the evening; have no Bibles or Testaments in the village. A Koordish chief, Ezdesher Bey, came and plundered the village, and carried away all their Testaments and religious books.

"SABBATH, NOV. 30, 1856.

"Mansoria, a Nestorian village. A clear and cloudless morning. Have a splendid view over the river, and the hills round about from the house-top. The priest calls to see us, a pleasant, amiable man. Present him with a copy of the Ingil in Chaldean and Syriac. Shemmas Eremiah reads and explains it to him. He says it is very good and he receives it with much gratitude and thankfulness.

"Then we assemble the villagers in the church with the priest, and give them the open Gospel, and tell them to read it, and follow its teachings to guide them to heaven. Tell them to believe the Bible, have faith in Christ, and pray for the Holy Spirit to dwell in their hearts and sanctify them unto everlasting life. They pay most devout attention and frequently respond 'Yes, yes, it is true.'

"It is most interesting to preach to these poor, oppressed Christians, who believe in Christ, on the banks of the ancient Tigris. Entreat them to pray that Moslems, Nestorians, Jacobites, Yezidees, all may receive the same Gospel and become brothers together in Christ Jesus. The dress of the women; white head-dress, loose robe, long braid to the hair, bracelets and beads on their arms, and anklets on their feet, and many silver coins on their head and neck. The men wear a conical felt cap, bound around with a red figured turban. In the afternoon they came to the Hakem for medicine, and are very friendly. At sunset see the ground where the great battle between Beder Khan Bey and Reschid Pasha was fought. A Koordish chief, who plundered the Christian villages, and was taken captive by the Turks, is now a prisoner in the island of Crete.

"Also look over to Mount Judy, where Noah's ark is said to have rested, a high mountain, covered with snow. Beyond, near Elkosh, is Am Sifna where tradition relates that Noah built his ark.

"In the evening the priest comes from Shah, the bishop feared to come because he thought we might make him Catholic or Protestant. Isaac, the teacher, comes with him, who has been instructed in Oroomiah by Mr. Stoddard; give to Isaac a Testament to carry to Maraha, a Nestorian village, two hours distant, about 150 population, fifteen can read; they very much desire a Bible, send also a Bible and Gospel by the Priest Isaiah to the Nestorian bishop, Mar Joseph, at Shah, a village six hours distant, 200 population; send also a letter to testify that American Christians love much the Nestorians and desire them all to receive the Bible and Gospel of salvation. We dine upon a young kid of a goat. A girl sits at the outer door with a dish of porridge in her hand to give some from a spoon to all the poor who come to receive it. Shemmas Eremiah is very entertaining in conversation. Koordish proverb, 'If he see me I am friend, if he not see me I am thief.' Nestorian prayer in church, glory to God in the highest, on earth peace, good will to men, then the Lord's Prayer. Cry from the minaret, Alla hou achbar, twice repeated, Allah la il Allah, etc. The Catholics come in the evening and we preach the truth to them.

"MONDAY, Dec. 1.

"Attend the Nestorian prayer in the morning before sunrise. The priest alone, in a dark room, repeats them from memory; two prayers and five or six psalms. He can repeat all the Psalms by heart. One old woman comes, none of the people. We ride to Jesireh, have much detention in crossing the river; find there a new Moodir, Sadik Agha, a fine-looking, energetic man, who receives us with much politeness. The Medghis come in, Cadi, and various dignitaries, ten in number; 2,000 population, 1,500 Moslems, 500 Christians.

"Meet with Lord Henry Ker, of the English embassy to Persia, travelling by post, and bearer of despatches to Diarbekir and Aleppo. He dines with us in Anglo-Turkish style. We then bid farewell to our friends, Shemmas and the Doctor, and ride in company with his Lordship two hours upon the road. He is a very affable and pleasant gentlemen, twenty years of age, and has travelled much in the East. We ride two hours longer over a very stony road, and arrive just at sunset at the Koordish village of Hemdik; 10 houses, 50 population; situated in the midst of the plain, bounded by snow-crowned mountains.

"TUESDAY, 2.

"Have a splendid sunrise view from our house-top over Mount Judy, where tradition relates that Noah's ark rested, and the dove plucked the olive branch from the plain.

"In one hour came to the village of Babin, an old ruined town. The Onbashi refuses us a horseman. We continue our way past two small Koordish villages, over a wretchedly rough, rocky road, and lunch at noon on a little green spot in sight of the village of Ainser. Just before sunset arrive at Deir Ona. The Moodir is holding his medghis in the open air, clothed in a scarlet cloak. He is very civil—says he will give me horsemen, and begs me not to report the *Onbashi* to the Pasha, who dishonored the Sultan's firman—One hundred and fifty population, Moslems and Jacobites. Hadji Suleiman Agha, very civil—comes himself on his fast horse, one half hour, to make ready a konak for us.

"We spend the night at the Koordish village of Atim—forty population; ten Jacobites.

"WEDNESDAY, 3.

"We are in the saddle at sunrise; in one hour we cross the plain with the Sinjar hills on our left and the Marian mountain on our right, and the vast (chul) desert stretching before us, we come to the village Bannet, on a little mound—one hundred and fifty Jacobites, Armenians, and Moslems. The villages are all upon raised mounds; peasants are ploughing and sowing in the fields, and the land is productive.

"The white church of Nisilin is seen in the morning sunlight far away.

"We lunch at noon in sight of the snow-crowned mountains just rising above the wide spreading plain like peaks of light and purity exceedingly beautiful. A raised mound gives us a splendid view in all directions; stop at the village. The Kahya *Shukuro* is very polite and cordial in his greetings and attention. We then gallop on across the plain, passed several mound-built villages, and in two hours come in sight of the large barrack of Nisilin. Mule falls sick on the way; treatment and tears of muleteers. Meet several troops of soldiers, a Koordish chief with his guard —see the women coming to the wells with their rope to draw water; arrive at sunset across the river Chebar at Nisilin. Again we see another river where the Prophet Ezekiel is said to have seen the sublime visions of Jehovah and his glory

We find a curious room full of soldiers seated round a good fire, smoking and drinking coffee. Call upon the nakie of Moodir; send for the Usbashi, and dispatch two horsemen for our mules. Have a long konak, and comfortable quarters fòr the night.

"THURSDAY, 4.

"See the ancient river Chebar from the house-top winding far through the plain. We ride two hours over the plain. On the left partly desert, on the right cultivated land, and arrive at the ruined barracks, Russer *Sercha Rhan*. A few miserable Arabs are quarrelling over their measures of barley; a half dozen stone huts filled with women and children are inclosed within the ancient walls.

"We lunch to-day upon the open plain. Then in two hours we come to *Dara*. It is well situated on a hillside in front of the great plain, and beside a stream of pure water.

"Here are extensive old Roman ruins, temples, theatres, bridges, immense blocks of hewn stone, and all the marks of their ancient power. Also many tombs and sepulchres cut in the rock. Two hours more over hill and valley bring us at sun-set to the village of *Harin;* three hundred and fifty population—all Arabs, who spend the winter in their houses here, and in summer take their tents and flocks, and go out into the desert. The

Kahaya *Seid Hassein* is a good specimen of the Arab character; invite him to come to England; have a pleasant talk with him in the evening. The Shammar Sinjar and *Anasee*, occupy the whole of the desert to Baghdad and Damascus. He says the Sinjar are no more; they have become *Yezidee.* The village is situated near an old mound, and beside a well and running water. See a large caravan of camels coming in the evening to rest here.

"FRIDAY, 5.

"Beautiful morning; see women and girls drawing water from the well with their own ropes, to water the mules and camels, as in Scripture days, in ancient Mesopotamia.

"We then ride across the fertile plain to the mountain side. Mardin rises high above us with a castle fortress higher still. The air is pure and bracing. The son of the Kahya, mounted on his fine Arab horse, performs feats of horsemanship in curves and circles around us. Climbing over the rugged, rocky ascent in one hour, we come to the convent Deir Zafetran, the residence of the Patriarch of the Jacobite Church, in the East, Patriarch Jacob. It is beautifully and securely situated, commanding a wide view over the plain and desert. There is good water, cistern, well, fountain, springs. Grapes and figs are cultivated, and wheat and barley. The Patriarch and his vakel are absent. Two of his Rahab and Shemmas, Priests and Deacons, receive us very kindly and provide us with eggs, cheese and bread for refreshment. They show us through the convent, and to the church. It is adorned with red-colored paintings of the Saviour, the Apostles, Saints, and the Virgins upon the walls. They do not worship these as do the Catholics, but pray to Christ alone. They have a large silver gilt Gospel before the high altar. I find a copy of the Bible in Arabic and Syrian here.

"They pray seven times a day, and spend the remainder of their time in writing manuscripts. They pray at midnight and before sunrise, midday and sunset; three times in the church. The wooden bell, struck with a large stick, sounds the hour for prayers at noon. We attended the service in the church. They cross themselves, bow down, chant their prayer from a book, then draw aside the curtain from before the high altar, where a lamp is burning, then cross and prostrate themselves, and chant a short prayer again. The chapel is hung round with glass and gilded lamps. They all go forward and kiss the cover of the Gospel and the stone of St. John. They listen with much interest and with tears in their eyes to our spiritual conversation, after service. We tell them they must pray for the Holy

Spirit to guide them in the way of all truth. The Saviour promised to his disciples to give them the Comforter, to dwell within them unto everlasting life. They must pray not only with the lips, but with the heart. A very interesting visit. We then came into a smooth winding path among the hills (stone churches cut in the rocks, rise high above), and in one half hour we arrive at the Jacobite village of Kala Mora (Woman Castle). High above is a strong castle held by a woman against Tamerlane the Great, until he retired from its walls. A few minutes more bring us in sight of Mardin, a strong walled city on the mountain side, overlooking the plain and desert that stretches 280 miles towards the south. A strong fortified and strongly guarded castle commands the whole. Mardin has a population of 10,000; 5,000 Moslems; 2,000 Jacobites; 2,000 Armenians; 400 Chaldeans; 500 Assyrians; 100 Jews. We are met at the gate by a cavass, who conducts us to the house of Howadji *Yuseph*, a Catholic Armenian of large wealth. He receives us very hospitably into an elegantly carpeted and cushioned room, and makes every effort to contribute to our entertainment. The Pasha also sends his Usbashi (major) to meet and accompany us to the Ronak, and inquire what is our wish. Then we pay him a visit at the house of Suleiman Agha (Caimakan). Aali Pasha receives us with great courtesy. He is a noble, soldier-like man, of much personal presence. He was engaged in the war on the Danube and at Kars. He is a great friend of General Williams and the English. We tell him that our journey thus far in the Turkish empire, from Stamboul, has been very agreeable, as we have a great firman from the Sultan. We have been treated with much politeness by all the Pashas, Moodirs, and officers of the Sultan. Only one Usbashi have we met with who said he did not know the Sultan Abdul Medjid or his firman; neither did he care for the Pasha, and he would give us no guard. He immediately sends for his usbashi, (major) and orders the corporal to be removed from office, arrested, and brought to Mardin in irons. Thus summarily is justice dispensed in Turkey. He was dressed in Frank style, and very cordial in his manner.

"Returning thence, the Jacobite bishop (Matran Joseph) calls upon us. A fine-looking, benevolent, venerable man, very like the archbishop of Mosul. He loves much the Bible, is well instructed in the Scriptures, and desires all his people to have the Bible. It comes from God, tells us of Jesus Christ and the Gospel of salvation, and guides us to heaven.

"We tell him if we both pray for the holy spirit to dwell in our hearts, we may hope to meet in heaven.

"We then go out to take a Turkish bath. Our host has it all made ready, clean, and scented with incense. We are greatly refreshed, and return with a good appetite for dinner. Our host dines with us at his round table, loaded with various and excellent dishes, pilaff, meats, peaches, etc. We have pleasant spiritual conversation at dinner; he seems to be a true Christian at heart. He is a noble specimen of an Armenian gentleman, dressed in a fur robe, with black hair and eyes, intelligent and affable. He wishes to send his children to America, or England to be educated. He is an adopted son of the Sultan, and all his property falls into his hand when he dies. He is also the head of all the Rayahs in the city.

"Our beds are made in comfortable style, and we retire very agreeably for the night.

"Saturday 6.

"A magnificent morning. The Aali Pasha and the Carmakan Suleiman Agha call upon us this morning at our konak. We have a very pleasant visit with his Excellency; he is exceedingly courteous and polite. A fine, commanding man. Our host accompanied us on horseback without the walls of the city. The road is more steep, rugged, and rocky beyond description. In two hours and a half we lunch on the sunny mountain side, near a stream of cool water, and have before us a wide-reaching view of the surrounding landscape."

These were probably the last words that Mr. Righter wrote. On this day he complained of being unwell, and in a few days he was no more.

The following was found in his coat pocket after his death, and was broken off like his own career, in the midst:

"MOSUL, ASIA MINOR, Nov. 14, 1856.

"MY DEAR MOTHER: How greatly we have enjoyed our visit to this distant missionary station, on the river Tigris, near the city of Nineveh, to which Jonah preached at the command of the Lord; and they repented in sackcloth and ashes, and 'God repented of the evil that he had said that he would do unto them and did it not,' but afterwards overthrew the city for their sins with terrible destruction.

"The good missionary brethren have given us almost an angel's welcome in this far-off land. Yesterday we rode out to visit the ruins of Nineveh, that was destroyed by fire, and is now buried beneath the crumbling earth of sun-dried brick. The gateways, palaces, and temples have been excavated in deep trenches. We descended underground into these, and there saw the huge, human-headed winged bulls, standing where they were worshipped, at the entrance of the palace temple.

" We saw also the battle scenes of the ancient Assyrians traced upon the walls of their temples: the king in his chariot, the discharge of arrows, the conflict and victory, and the captives brought from far. The siege, too, of a walled city, the towers, battlements, and palm-trees of ancient Tyre, that was conquered by the Assyrians. The cuneiform, arrow-headed, ancient writing, describing these scenes, was also traced upon the blocks of stone underneath. It was most interesting to see with——

CHAPTER XXI.

LAST ILLNESS AND DEATH.

WHILE Mr. Righter was making the entry in his note-book with which the preceding chapter closes, he was suffering from the attack of disease which terminated his valuable life. No account of this last illness could be given in such fitting and expressive language as that which is contained in the letters of his travelling companion, Rev. Mr. Jones, and of the missionaries at Diarbekir, where it pleased God, in the great kindness of his providence, that his life should be terminated. Nowhere upon the face of the earth, save in the home of his parents, could he have breathed out his life with more tender evidences of the loving-kindness of his heavenly Father, into whose home he was taken. He died literally in the midst of brethren and sisters, and all the offices which long love could have performed were bestowed upon him. The letter of Dr. Nutting, at whose house he died, gives a full account of his last illness, and this is first quoted:

LETTER FROM REV. DAVID H. NUTTING, M.D.

"DIARBEKIR, ASSYRIA, December 16th, 1856.

"To the Parents, Brothers, and Sisters of
"the late Rev. C. N. RIGHTER.

"DEAR FRIENDS—A sad duty now devolves upon me: I am to undertake to give you an account of the last sickness of your son and brother. You will have learned from the letter of Rev. Mr. Jones, his companion in travel, that Mr. R. did not consider himself sick until the 6th instant, the day they left Mardin, a city about fifty miles south of this, although he had for two or three weeks previous had little appetite, and sometimes complained of chilliness. At their noon lunch that day, when he made his last entry in his journal, he complained of being very chilly, although he had three coats on, and was sitting in the sun, and had his servant hold an umbrella to protect him from the wind. From that place they had ridden on only about two hours, when, as Mr. R. still felt cold and somewhat ill, it was thought best that they turn aside to a village, called *Zahnkir*, to spend the night and Sabbath. They hoped that by taking some thoroughwort or sage tea to induce perspiration that night, and resting the next day, he would be well and able to proceed to Diarbekir on Monday the 8th. But Monday came, and he was not well: had suffered much pain in right side and shoulder, and had some feverishness. Mr. Jones administered some medicine to him (very suitable to his condition, I think), and it operated favorably, and the next morning he was much better. It was decided that Mr. Jones go on with one servant and zabtier to Diarbekir that day (and inform me of Mr. R.'s sickness, so that I could go down to meet him), leaving Mr. R., with the other servant, and zabtier, and carterjees, to start on two or three hours after sunrise, when the morning frost would have disappeared. He hoped to be able to proceed five or six hours that day, and the following to reach this city. That evening Mr. Jones came, and to our great surprise Mr. R. came not with him. He immediately told us that he left Mr. R. ill a few hours out, but that he was much better that morning, and hoped he would be able to. come easily the one day's journey in *two.*

"In the morning, after breakfast, with our good Deacon Shimas, I rode down the river on the road to Mardin, hoping to meet Mr. Righter three or four hours from the city. It was a clear, lovely day, like pleasant October days in N. E., and the road was excellent. We had proceeded about three and one half hours, when we met Mr. Righter's servant, carterjees, and baggage. We asked where Mr. R. was. They said he had gone on before with the cavass or zabtier, and were surprised that we had not met him. We concluded he had taken another road, and turning, followed on after him. At the village of 'Cahby-kir' we overtook him. He had stopped to rest a few moments, and was standing before a house with a crowd of natives around him. As I rode up I was struck with his unusual slowness in greeting me. He did not seem particularly weak, but spoke and moved like a man benumbed with cold. He said he had come very easily, and was not much fatigued. He was sipping a little brandy and water, which he said he found much to refresh him. I asked him if he would not go into a house and lie down awhile before proceeding. He thought it unnecessary and not desirable, particularly as it might make us late in reaching the city. Soon we mounted and rode quietly on. He was on an Arab horse, which he bought in Mosul, and which he said carried him with very little motion and jar. He was very glad to be informed that several letters for him had arrived since he went to Mosul, and said he had anticipated having a feast of letters when he reached Diarbekir. When we were about a mile and a half from the city we were met by Mr. Walker and Mr. Jones, whom he was much pleased to see, and thanked for coming to meet him.

"It was nearly four o'clock when we reached

my house. We took him immediately up into our parlor, and he sat for awhile by the stove in the rocking chair, before having his overcoats, riding boots, and hat taken off, fearing he might take cold if his outer clothing was removed too suddenly. He then walked about the room a minute or two, and, at my request, laid down upon a lounge. Soon I brought the letters to him, and he looked them all over, and said he knew from whom each one came, by the handwriting and postmarks. He then laid them aside saying he was then too much fatigued to read them. Mrs. N. then brought him a cup of tea and soda crackers, and he sat up by the table. I had brought to him also a wash-bowl, etc., but he seemed not to have resolution sufficient either to wash, or take the tea even; and requested me to allow them to stand by him a little while. After sitting awhile he seemed to revive, washed, drank his tea, and proposed to go down to dine with us, but did not go, as I thought it would be too much for him in his exhausted state. Soon I asked him to the bed-room adjoining the parlor, and he laid down saying he felt very grateful for such a comfortable bed and pleasant room. I was with him all the evening, and though he did not sleep, he seemed to be resting. He had considerable fever, as he said he had had for three or four nights previous. At 11 o'clock he thought he needed nothing more and should sleep: and as Mr. Jones was to sleep in the same room, and his servant in an adjoining one, he said it was entirely unnecessary for me to sit up longer, and he begged I would retire. I did so.

"Early in the morning (*Thursday*) I went to his room and he seemed much better, had slept considerable, and his fever had abated. He continued thus till 10 o'clock, when he began to have pain, first in his side, then in his back, and then all over. He said, 'Doctor, something is wrong—something has given way within.' Soon he was relieved of the pain, and seemed quite easy. I was with him all the forenoon, endeavoring to ascertain as definitely as possible, the nature and state of his disease. I at first suspected it might be disease of the liver; and upon examination I found there was a slight enlargement, just below the ribs on the right side. Not long before now, as I was sitting by him, he said, 'Doctor, I think I ought to tell you I am deranged; but you need not mention it to others.' I thought that perhaps want of sleep and nervous exhaustion had brought his mind into such a state, and that it would soon pass away. A little before noon I had occasion to leave the room for a few minutes, and upon returning I found Mr. Jones sprinkling water into his face. He said that Mr. R. was taken with shivering and trembling, and seemed to faint.

As I came up to the bed, I saw he was still trembling, and his lips were moving as if in prayer. Just then he seemed to faint, saying, 'I am going, I am going.' I applied some spirits of camphor to his nose, and he revived, saying, 'Lord, I will repent.' The servant told me that while I was out before noon, Mr. R. was much engaged in earnest prayer. For six or eight hours from this time he answered none of our questions, although he turned his eyes sometimes towards the person who addressed him. All this time I was with him, and felt exceedingly anxious for him. I looked upon the shivering I had seen as an indication that the inflammation of the liver had resulted in suppuration, and an abscess was being formed; and then he could not probably live many days. I thought that he probably, too, had a presentiment that his time was short, and that he was endeavoring by meditation and prayer to secure a preparation for the great change that awaited him, and during these hours, many, many were the prayers I offered that our heavenly Father would be near to comfort and sustain him as he approached the valley of the shadow of death. In the evening he had several naps, and each one in succession longer than the one preceding. At nearly ten o'clock he awoke from a quiet sleep of more than half-an-hour, and seemed to be himself again. He said he had been in a *trance*. He had known all that we had said to him but was unable to answer our questions.' We then moved him into the parlor, where we had prepared a bed for him. He sat up nearly a half hour, and conversed quite freely, and then laid down. He seemed very comfortable, and said, 'All is peace and joy.' At a late hour I left him, with one of his faithful servants to watch with him, and Mr. Jones sleeping in the same room. He had not as much fever as the previous night, and slept considerable. Next morning (*Friday*) at five o'clock I went in to see him, and he said, 'Doctor, I have had some refreshing sleep, and am much better, will you please to bring me those letters from my dear friends, I think I am able to read them now.' I brought them, and he opened and read them all, excepting one, which he said he knew contained nothing but a draft on Baring Brothers, I think. In the letters from his two brothers he seemed much interested; and he told me they contained good news from his far-off home—which to him was like cold water to a thirsty man. After breakfast, we had family prayers in the parlor, and he seemed to enjoy the season very much. A portion of Scripture having been read, he united with us in singing the 402d hymn of the 'Temple Melodies,' commencing:

"'How firm a foundation, ye saints of the Lord,
Is laid for your faith in his excellent word.'

As he sang the last verse I could but feel that no one could sing it with the heartfelt confidence he evinced, unless he had in exercise a strong and living faith in Christ. That day Mr. R. appeared so decidedly better, that we began to hope that my previous conclusion in regard to his disease was incorrect, and that he would recover. I think also that *he* had hope that he would soon be well. Mr. Jones was very anxious to prosecute the journey as soon as possible; and he asked Mr. R. if he should contract with a muleteer to be ready to start with them on the following Monday for Aintab. He replied, 'Yes, I think it would be well to do so.' That night he had more fever than during the day, but not as much as the first nights; and during the greater part was in a gentle perspiration; yet he was rather restless and did not sleep, as I hoped he would. *Saturday* morning, instead of finding him better than the previous day, he did not appear quite as well, and our hopes were somewhat lessened. In answer to Mr. Jones' inquiry, he said that the contract had better be made for Tuesday instead of Monday. His fever began to appear more like a hectic than a remittent fever. Still he seemed very cheerful and hopeful. That evening, thinking that it was very important that he should sleep, I gave him a powder of morphine.

"*Sabbath* morning, when I asked him how he

was, he replied, 'much better, Doctor, I slept a part of the night, and oh! it was such a refreshing sleep! I am all right now, Doctor—all right.' Not long after this, as he was apparently waking from a nap, I heard him utter these words, 'Who doeth all things well.' He slept considerable during the A.M. In the P.M. he said he thought a warm bath would do him good. I was then just going to meeting and told him that, on my return, I would see about his having a bath. When I returned from our place of worship I found he had ordered the servants to bring hot water, etc., and had taken his bath. He told me it was the most delightful bath he had ever taken, 'Such pleasurable physical sensations.' Mr. and Mrs. Walker called in after meeting, and he seemed very happy to see them. He said that that had been the happiest Sabbath of his life—'So quiet, so peaceful, so joyous, so glorious.' Soon after he heard us inviting Mr. Jones to preach that evening to the members of this station, and he said, 'O yes, friend Jones, *do* give them a sermon!'

"Mr. Jones, Mr. and Mrs. Walker, Mr. and Mrs. Knapp, Mrs. Nutting and myself, met in our dining room at 7 o'clock; and after the usual introductory exercise conducted by Mr. Jones, he preached a very excellent sermon from the seventh verse of the 57th Psalm. After that we sang several hymns, accompanied by the melodeon. In the meantime Mr. R. was attended by the two servants. At nine o'clock I went up to his room and found him apparently very happy and inclined to talk much. I told him we had enjoyed our meeting exceedingly, and felt sorry he was unable to be with us. I asked him how he had been. 'In a delightful state, Doctor; oh, such glorious views as I have had!' Soon he began to sing—

"'Awake my soul, stretch every nerve,' etc.

and parts of several other similar hymns. I noticed that he appeared very much excited, and threw his arms about in a restless, nervous way, and I was not long in coming to the conclusion that he was delirious. We tried to keep him calm and quiet, but he grew worse for several hours. Mr. J. and Mrs. N. were up till after midnight, and (with two servants) I was standing by him all night. Frequently, after a few moments of sleep, he would break out in singing, or would speak as if preaching, or making an address. Once or twice he said, 'Oh, I see the glory of the Divine Nature, nearer and nearer it comes —how beautiful—how *glorious!*' The latter part of the night he began to be more quiet, and in the morning, *Monday*, he slept considerable; and during the day he seemed nearly free from delirium, and always answered our questions intelligently. His pulse was quicker and weaker than the preceding day, owing, I thought, in part, at least, to the excitement of the night before. Towards evening, Mr. Jones having gone over to Mr. Walker's, Mr. R. requested me to send for him, and said he had something to tell him. 'I want to tell him of the glory of God.' In the evening Mr. Walker came, and kindly offered to sit up with Mr. R. that night, and give me an opportunity to rest. Having given direction in regard to the medicine to be given, before 10 I retired. Just before Mr. R. requested Mr. W. to wind up his watch. During the night he was somewhat delirious, but not nearly as much so as the preceding night. He was in a gentle perspiration most of the time, and in the morning, at 5 o'clock, when I came into the room, he seemed very quiet, but extremely sensitive to cold, and frequently repeated the words—'keep me warm—keep me warm.' I found his pulse much weaker than it was the preceding day. He said he had no pain, and was very easy and quiet. After breakfast, as I was by him, I inquired whether any of the letters he had just received were from his father or mother; and he said there was no letter from them, but two were from his brothers, and when he became stronger he would write to them. I told him I would not tire him with questions, for he needed rest. 'Yes,' he replied, 'after I have rested awhile, I shall be better.' Sometimes he would say—'God is good;' and several times he prayed—'Lord, deal gently with thy servant.' He continued quiet, and sleeping much of the time till half past-ten. I was with him all the time, and knew he was gradually growing weaker, but did not think he would leave us so soon as he did. I found at that time his pulse no longer perceptible, and his breathing was short though easy. I went and told Mr. Jones that I feared he would not be long with us, and when I returned to the bedside, I found his eyes open and fixed. I spoke to him, but he made no reply, though he continued to breathe till about eleven, when his spirit quietly left the frail body, and soared away to the blessed mansion where sickness, suffering, and sorrow are no more. So his prayer was answered. The Lord did deal gently with him, and his end was perfect peace. I have not time now, my dear friends, to write more. I deeply sympathize with you in your loss. I, as well as the others of our station, became very much interested in Mr. Righter; we loved him as our brother. We still love to think of him as our brother—a brother not lost, but before us gone to a happy land, where after a few years, at longest, we hope again to meet, and never part."

LETTER FROM REV. GEORGE C. KNAPP.

"DIARBEKIR, TURKEY, Wednesday, Dec. 17, 1856.

"DEAR AFFLICTED FRIENDS: You will learn from the particulars of accompanying letters from other members of this mission station of the Board such intelligence as will cause your heart to bleed! Dear friends, it is a sad as well as an unexpected task that we are called upon, by the inscrutable ways of Providence, to perform, while we think what must be the anguish of spirit we shall occasion to each one who reads! May the Lord grant you his grace to comfort and strengthen your hearts under the present bereavement.

"Yes, your beloved son and brother, Chester N. Righter is no more! This day it has been our mournful duty to commit his remains to the grave!

"Little did we think eight weeks ago when he spent several days with us, the very picture of health, exhibiting so freely his characteristic cheerfulness and resolution, that we should ever be called to perform so sad a duty! *Here* ended his earthly pilgrimage in a twofold sense. How true that the Lord's ways are not our ways, and it is not in man to direct his steps.

"In anticipation of your wishes to learn the particulars respecting the burial services of our departed brother, I will endeavor to give you them as faithfully as my time will admit.

"Our brother died about noon of yesterday; and we chose to depart from the established custom of this people of burying the dead on the same day of their decease, that we might make the desired arrangements without confusion.

"Owing to this mission station being in its infancy no Protestant burial-place has been secured; but our good deacon, Shemmas Sulleba, kindly offered us a space owned by him in the Syrian burying-ground. To feel secure from my fears of dissatisfaction the bishops and patriarch of that church were consulted, and they had no objection to his being buried there, if Shemmas was willing.

"Two of the best carpenters in the city were furnished by the English Consul, by whom they were employed, who made the coffin of unusually fine boards from Erzroum, which, fortunately, Brother Walker had purchased a year ago. It was made of the same shape common in America; and, according to the English custom, covered with fine black cloth. The inside was trimmed with white cambric, very tastefully plaited by our ladies. In this the body was deposited, and becomingly attired, according to the American custom.

"And now imagine yourselves seated with us in Dr. Nutting's spacious sitting-room. It is one o'clock. P.M. In the east end of the room, seated on a sofa, is H.B.M.'s Consul, Mr. Holmes, who, with his lady, had come to mingle his sympathies with ours; Major Gardin, an English officer, but now a tourist and the Consul's guest; Mr. Mattrass, the Consul's Secretary, and Dr. Nutting; while at their right is Rev. A. Walker; Rev. Mr. Jones, from England, and Secretary of the Turkish Missions' Aid Society, and myself; and opposite us three are the ladies, Mrs. Holmes, Walker, Nutting, and Knapp.

"This number probably constitute all the Franks speaking English in this city. Nearly in the centre of the room stands the table upon which are the sacred remains; and the other half of the room is crowded with the Protestant brethren and others. In the spacious court before us are several hundred persons, as also many are on the roofs of the house, all anxious to witness the funeral of a foreigner.

"The religious exercises were as follow:

"1. Singing the first twelve verses of the 90th Ps. to a chant.

"2. Prayer by the writer.

"3. An excellent and appropriate address by Rev. Henry Jones, based on Ps. xc. 12.

"4. Address by Rev. Mr. Walker in Turkish.

"5. Prayer by Rev. Mr. Walker in Turkish.

"6. Singing, 'I would not live alway.'

"The above exercises occupied a little over an hour. The remains were then borne on a hearse by sixteen of the most prominent men of the Protestant community. These were preceded by two cavasses furnished by the Pasha as a mark of respect; after the bearers were the Consul's two cavasses. Then followed on horseback Rev. Mr. Jones, the Consul, Maj. Gardin, Mr. Mattrass, Rev. W., myself, Dr. S., and Harji Hargoss, the Consul's Interpreter, and member of our church. Then followed a large concourse of people, as we proceeded through the main street leading to the western gate. The ladies had taken another street more retired and unobtrusive.

"Twenty minutes brought us to the gate, and passing through we turned to the left, passing along some ten or twelve rods under the high walls, after which, a sharp bend to the right, winding our way mostly among the prostrate tomb-stones about twenty rods, brought us to the newly-prepared grave.

"The weather was mild and serene, and there being no snow to be seen, the heavens being clear, it resembled a genial day in spring.

"The exercises at the grave were:

"1st. Singing, 'There is an hour of peaceful rest.'—Tune, Woodland.*

* These three tunes we found in the "Temple Melodies.'

"2d. Prayer by Rev. Mr. W.

"3d. Prayer in Turkish by one of our church members.

"4th. Benediction by Rev. Mr. W. in Turkish.

"The grave of ample dimensions, between seven and eight feet deep, in the hard, red-clay soil, then received its sacred trust. Under and about the coffin, upon which was placed a firm construction of boards, was deposited a large quantity of charcoal, to render more feasible disinterment should it ever be desired.

"There were several hundred spectators, and throughout the whole day there was perfect order.

"*Our task was done!* But oh! what an impressive lesson to mortal man! Here is one, who a few days since had as good a prospect of a long life as any of us, possessing apparently a firm, robust constitution, but now numbered with the dead! Let this teach the frailty of man. Let this people, as they reflect upon the noble mission of our faithful departed brother, in furnishing them the lamp of eternal life, consider how much efforts for their salvation do cost, and likewise the additional guilt of refusing that Gospel thus costing so much sacrifice of life. May we, who are permitted to remain here awhile longer, improve by this sad event, seeking to have our hearts sanctified, becoming more faithful in our

Master's service, and better prepared when he shall summon us hence.

"Your affectionate
Brother in Christ,
"GEO. C. KNAPP."

LETTER FROM REV. DR. SCHAUFFLER.

"BEBEK, CONSTANTINOPLE, January 15, 1857.

"MR. RIGHTER—Very Dear Sir: The relation which I sustained to your beloved son, now no more among the 'pilgrims and strangers' of this world, leads me to send you an expression of my heartfelt sympathy with you in your heavy bereavement. Your son was our next door neighbor, constantly in our family circle, of which he was almost a regular member. In days of sickness he knew he could freely call upon us, as for parental sympathy and care; and in his many and useful labors, he consulted with me as an older laborer in this field. When he left us, he committed to me the Records, etc., of the Evangelical Alliance, of which he was the first Secretary, and it was my solemn duty to convoke the first committee meeting after his decease—to communicate to them the intelligence of our sad bereavement, and to propose the resolutions relative to his death, and the choice of another secretary.

Your dear son was beloved by all who knew him, and his usefulness, his zeal for the glory of God and the good of souls, was manifest to all. Even the Greek family with whom he lived (a plain poor family), appreciated his worth, loved him as a member of their household, and served him, especially in days of illness, with a tenderness which showed that their *hearts*, not their pecuniary interest, dictated their conduct. I was the more delighted to see this, as it is so rare a thing to get the true, heartfelt affections of this nation. When the news of his death came, our servant girls, returning from their humble habitation, remarked 'They are crying themselves sick over there, because Mr. R. is no more.' And so I found them afterwards, sorrowing as for a brother. Perhaps you may improve, some time, an opportunity to send them *some trifle of an object* as a recognition of their kindness to your dear son. *A small thing* would be of great value to them, given on Mr. R.'s account, and lead them to feel that their humble and unostentatious affection for their friend was appreciated, and encourage them in cultivating the better sensibilities of human nature. You will excuse this suggestion, which is made under the impression that such small gifts are a blessing to him that gives, and to him that receives, far, far beyond its pecuniary value, which in such cases quite vanishes out of sight.

"We have been in the room of your son to see what he left behind. We find that he lived as 'a pilgrim and stranger on the earth.' There are, however, objects enough that will interest his parents and other friends, and they shall be sent to you faithfully—viz. his remaining clothes, and the articles he made daily or frequent use of, and some curiosities he had gathered. I found three books written full with pencil, like notes by the way, or diaries. I have not examined them, nor shall I do so, as they may contain subjects of a private character. You will receive them unread by any one, if Providence brings the box to you in safety.

"And now, my dear sir, feeling somewhat acquainted with you and Mrs. R., from having seen several times your daguerreotypes (now with several others in my keeping), I cannot but express to you that this affliction may be so blest and sanctified to you and your dear family, as that you shall, one and all, devote yourselves to the same Saviour whom your departed son loved and served, and whom he now beholds and will behold forever. I am sure, no member of your dear family will take it ill, if an old missionary friend of their sainted son and brother beseeches them to prepare by faith in Christ, for a happy meeting with the dear one they will never again see on earth, in a better world, where, 'those that meet shall part no more, and those long parted meet again.' Be ye likewise ready, for in an hour when ye think not, the Son of Man will come. How happy, if on that day, when the Lord Jesus shall make up his jewels, you will be found then, none wanting, an unbroken, undiminished family, never to weep again. The Lord that gave *him grace*, grant it to you all, and thus magnify in you all the riches of his grace.

"With kind, sympathizing remembrance to Mrs. R. and every member of your family,

"I remain, yours truly,

"W. G. SCHAUFFLER."

CHAPTER XXII.

TRIBUTES TO HIS MEMORY.

SOME of the tributes which have been paid to the memory of Mr. Righter will form an appropriate close to this volume. Those who have read the record of his life, as it has been sketched, will need no farther testimony to the strength of affection with which he was regarded by those who were intimately acquainted and associated with him, and to the loss which was sustained by the cause to which he had devoted himself. But it is proper that some of this testimony should be preserved.

The following letter was addressed to the Secretary of the American Bible Society, by Rev. Dr. Dwight, one of the Missionaries of the American Board in Turkey:—

"CONSTANTINOPLE, January 10, 1857.

"MY DEAR SIR:—By the last post letters were forwarded from this place to New York, and I think one at least to yourself, communicating the deeply afflictive intelligence of the early and sudden departure of our dearly beloved brother and fellow-laborer, and your Agent in Turkey, the Rev. Chester N. Righter. I find it impossible to make it appear a reality to my mind, he was so recently among us; was so young, so ardent, and energetic in his work, and apparently so necessary to all the good enterprises going forward in this land. But it is, alas! too true. We shall see his face and hear his voice no more, nor will he any longer aid us in bearing the burdens of the 'day (not 'night') of toil' in this land. He has been called to a higher service, and we would not that he should return to us, if that were possible. But we are permitted to mourn over our own bereavement, and over the loss that has been sustained by the good cause here, in consequence of his removal. And we are called upon to humble ourselves before the mighty hand of God, and confess our sins, that call for such rebukes and chastisements. We will also pray that He will soon send out other laborers to take the place of our dear brother and of others who have fallen in these whitened fields.

"I hope that your Committee will be early directed by Providence to another man, to appoint to fill the place thus vacated. Of its importance I need not speak, except to bear testimony, as one upon the ground, that there is plenty of work for such an agent to do.

"But to return to Mr. Righter: I think you will fell that your loss is a great one. This is the universal feeling here in regard to ourselves and this land. We had all become exceedingly attached to him. He was so kind in all his ways; so gentle in his spirit; so gentlemanly in his manners; so active, energetic, and persevering in every good word and work, and especially in his great work on which his whole heart was set, of disseminating as widely as possible, among all classes, the pure Word of God; that everybody admired and loved him.

"I am personally unacquainted with his parents and friends, but I beg through you to offer them my sincere condolence; and if it will be any comfort to them to read these few lines which I have penned in the sincerity of my heart, I beg that you will give them the opportunity.

"I take the liberty of enclosing for you and also for them, if you think it best, or for any other use you may think it proper to make of them, two letters received by me in reference to our dear young friend's death.

"It became my duty to announce the event to the Hon. Carroll Spence, our Minister at the Porte, and also to Rev. Horace M. Blakiston, the very worthy chaplain of the British Embassy here, and these are their replies. They will tell you in what esteem your late agent was held in this country.

"I remain, my dear Sir,
"Most truly and sincerely yours,
"H. G. O. Dwight.

"To the Secretary of the American Bible Society."

At the meeting of the Board of Managers of the American Bible Society, held March 5th, 1857, soon after the intelligence of his death was received, after appropriate remarks by the Rev. Dr. De Witt, the following minute and resolution were unanimously adapted:

"Intelligence having been received, since the last meeting, of the decease of the Rev. Chester N. Righter, the Society's Agent for Turkey and adjacent countries, the Managers would here record their deep sense of sorrow in the loss of this valued helper in our great Bible work. Their hopes of his usefulness, which were strong in the beginning of his labors, have been more than realized in his subsequent history. His communications from the Turkish capital, from Greece, from the Crimea, from Egypt, Palestine, Asia Minor, and lastly from Mesopotamia, all exhibit a union of good judgment, prudence, and industry, united with a modest, catholic piety, which have greatly endeared him to the

Board, and rendered his loss a trial. That the Board have not overvalued their deceased friend is made apparent by the sympathy manifested in his death at the various mission stations which he visited, and by other classes of men around him, both in public and private life.

"While the Managers, therefore, record their sorrow at the death of their worthy Agent, they would at the same time be grateful for the good which he was permitted to accomplish; also for the many kind attentions which he received in his last illness, and for the manifold expressions of regard for his memory in that ancient land where his labors and his life ended.

"*Resolved*, That a copy of the above record be transmitted to the relatives of the deceased, and to those missionary and other friends at the East who have shown so deep a sympathy in the loss sustained.

"COPY OF RESOLUTIONS PASSED AT A MEETING OF THE COMMITTEE OF THE CONSTANTINOPLE BRANCH OF THE EVANGELICAL ALLIANCE, HELD IN PERA, JANUARY 13TH, 1857.

"*Resolved*, That the news of the sudden death of the Rev. C. N. Righter has filled us with sorrow and dismay, and that we deeply deplore the loss of so useful a laborer in the Bible cause, and so active a member of this Committee.

"That while we bow with humble submission to the Divine will, we would express to the afflicted parents and friends of the deceased our sincere sympathy, commending them to the consolations of Divine Grace, and praying that they may all meet in Glory an unbroken family.

"That these resolutions be forwarded to the parents and friends of our lamented fellow-laborer in America."

The above resolutions were moved by the Rev. Dr. Schauffler, of the American mission, and after an expression on the part of the various members of the Committee present, of their high esteem for Mr. Righter, they were unanimously adopted.

Attest,
EDWIN E. BLISS,
Secretary.

CONSTANTINOPLE, Jan. 23, 1857.

FROM HON. CARROLL SPENCE, UNITED STATES MINISTER FOR TURKEY.

"CONSTANTINOPLE, Jan. 7, 1857.

"MY DEAR SIR: I have just received your note informing me of the unexpected decease of

Mr. Righter. The very kind personal relations which have existed between Mr. Righter and myself, since his stay in this empire, causes me to lament sincerely his untimely death. My intercourse with him for the last two years enabled me to form a correct opinion of his worth as a man, and his piety as a Christian; and while his bland and amiable manners secured for him my friendship, his zeal and energy in the prosecution of the pious task in which he was engaged elicited for him my sincere respect. Pious, without being austere—a sincere believer in the doctrines of the religion professed by him, without being intolerant—he gained the friendship and esteem of many, and avoided the enmity of all. His good common sense, his winning manners, his religious zeal, tempered by Christian charity towards all, his energy and perseverance of character, peculiarly fitted him to discharge the duties of the calling to which it was his intention to have devoted his life.

"Although his stay here has been short, his efforts in behalf of Christianity have been untiring, and the good he has done here, by the distribution of the Word of God, will remain behind him as a monument of his pious exertions, and will, as it developes itself in coming years, keep alive his memory in the recollection of those who were witnesses of his Christian labors.

"If it be a consolation to his relatives to learn that, in fighting the great battle of Christianity, he died upon the field of his struggle in its behalf, still longing to continue the conflict, that consolation is theirs; and may the knowledge of that fact, if it does not reconcile them to his loss, at least soothe them with the hope, that their loss in this world will be his gain in heaven.

"I beg you, should you write to his relatives, to unite my condolence with your own upon this melancholy occasion, and to express to them the deep regret I feel at the death of one for whom I entertained a sincere friendship.

"I am, my dear sir, truly yours,

"CARROLL SPENCE.

"Rev. H. G. O. DWIGHT, Constantinople."

Rev. Henry Jones, his travelling companion, writes:

"There was everything in his life and death calculated to afford comfort. He was a faithful and zealous servant of God, sincerely and earnestly desirous of promoting His glory and the salvation of souls by disseminating that gospel which is the power of God. As an agent of the American Bible Society, no one could labor more devotedly or with more untiring zeal. Wherever we journeyed, in every village, or city, or by the way, however wearied I might be, he lost no opportunity of promoting the most blessed object, so dear to his heart. Scarcely had we arrived at any mission station, when his inquiries would be for the Bible store, if there was one, and what arrangements could be made for the distribution of the Word of God, and his anxieties would never cease until he had accomplished his object. Nor did he confine his labors to those who were likely to appreciate them. He would spare no pains to obtain an entrance for the Bible when all others had failed to procure one. Well do I remember his dragging me over many weary miles to give the Bible to the Yezidees, or Devil-worshippers, and when he had succeeded, by dint of most judicious management and prayerful anxiety in obtaining a promise from the Yezidee chief and his priest, to read the Word of God, his joy was unbounded, and his prayers most fervent that God would bless it to the conversion and salvation of that benighted people. Such was his life; and his death, though it occurred in a far-off land and far away from the home of his fondest earthly affections, was attended with many circumstances which cannot fail to afford satisfaction and comfort to the friends who loved him so dearly."

The correspondent of the London *Christian Times* makes the following record of the event in a letter to that paper:

"CONSTANTINOPLE, Jan. 8, 1857.

"News has just reached this city of the sudden death of the Rev. C. N. Righter, at Diarbekir, on the 16th ult. He was the Agent of the American Bible Society in Turkey, and the Corresponding Secretary of the Constantinople Branch of the Evangelical Alliance. He left this place in September last, in company with the Rev. Henry Jones, Secretary of the Turkish Missions' Aid Society, for a tour in Asia Minor and Armenia, for the purpose of visiting all the missionary stations of the American Board. They proceeded as far as Mosul, and came, on their return, to Diarbekir, where Mr. Righter sickened of fever, and died within a very few days. He was, in many respects, a rare man, and his loss will be most deeply felt in this country and in America. He was, emphatically, 'a burning and a shining light,' laboring with untiring zeal, for the spread of God's Word among all classes of the population of Turkey, and at the same time endeavoring, by all means, to promote throughout this land the great objects of the Evangelical Alliance. And I may mention, for the interest it will excite in Britain, that during the war Mr. Righter was unwearied in his endeavors to furnish the soldiers of the allied armies, and also the Russian prisoners, with the Bible in their own vernacular tongue; and with this end in view, he even went to the Crimea, during that first winter of horrors, and was the means of administering comfort to many a poor, sick, and dying soldier, thus literally inheriting the 'blessing of him who was ready to perish.'"

The following was furnished to the *New York Observer* by Wm. C. Prime, Esq., Mr. Righter's travelling companion in Syria:—

"RECOLLECTIONS OF RIGHTER.

"My Dear Brother:—I feel deeply the loss of our friend Righter, and I cannot avoid giving you some of my personal recollections of him, as the companion of my last year's wanderings. He surprised me one evening at Thebes, by entering the cabin of my Nile boat, when I did not dream of an American being within a hundred or many hundred miles. My beard and bronzed face were as strange to him as his to me. We did not recognise each other.

"'I saw an American flag, and came over the river, hoping to meet an American,' said he.

"'You are right. I am from New York. My name is Prime.'

"'Is it possible? and mine is Righter.'

"I need not tell you my delight at this meeting. He passed the evening with me, and we talked over his adventures with you two years before, as we strolled by moonlight through the vast corridor of the temple of Luxor, under the side of which my boat lay.

"I met him again at Cairo, and he went with me to Jerusalem. It was not till after our arrival in the Holy City that he made up his mind to accept our invitation to join us for a few months of tent life on the hills of the Holy Land. He did at length join us, and was one of our little family of four who went wandering in the footsteps of the Lord and the Apostles last spring, and whom, as the companion of many thrilling scenes, I shall never forget until I forget Jerusalem.

"We bathed together in the Jordan, and in the Dead Sea; we studied together the page on which Abraham read the number of his children, as brilliant nowhere as it is above the oaks of Mamre; we were together cast away by a gale of wind on the Sea of Galilee; snowed under three days on the side of Mount Hermon; went to Damascus, to Baalbec, Beyrout, Tarsous, Rhodes, Smyrna and Constantinople together: and during all this time of constant hourly intercourse by day and night, there was no one word of jarring, no difference of plan, nor anything that I can now recal of him, other than the most entire amiability, warm-heartedness (if I may use the word), and earnestness of desire to make all of us happy. You will not think it strange that M—— and myself formed a warm attachment to him, and feel this affliction, as you said last week, like the loss of a brother.

"I remember with the utmost pleasure his constant cheerfulness. Nothing overcame it. First up in the morning, he would always make the air around the tents ring with a pleasant morning song, and when, as not unfrequently, our position was perilous or disheartening, he was never discouraged.

"His frank, hearty piety was always before us. He never yielded in a matter of duty one hair's-breadth. I remember especially the day of our approach to Damascus. It was Saturday. We had been under snow three days on Hermon, but determined this morning to reach the plain and the city if possible. As the sun was setting, my chief muleteer informed me that the mules could not go on. It was still eight miles to Damascus, of which the minarets and domes were shining in the red sunlight above its groves and gardens. I ordered a halt around the baggage, and soon found that it was probably impossible to reach the city. Righter alone differed from me, but solely on his own account. He had told me in starting with us, that he could not travel on Sunday, and such was my own intention also. I now regarded it as my duty to remain with the baggage, and come on to the city early on Sunday. There was none such on his part, and he hired a guide and a fresh horse, paying a guinea for the two, and set off alone for the city. I remember right well his cheerful face as he rode off that evening across the magnificent plain, waving his hand back to us as long as we could see him, and riding his horse as if he were born on horseback. He was the best horseman, for an American, that I have ever seen, riding always freely and gracefully.

"You have said nothing of your adventure at Nablous, in which he saved you from Bedouin spears. There was nothing in all my journey that pleased me more in Righter than his modesty at that spot. The Bedouins were again in commotion when we were there, and the Governor of Jerusalem, with two hundred men, was a close prisoner in the walls of Nablous, not daring to venture out to go to Jerusalem, on account of the state of the Arabs. We were unmolested here, though we had to show our pistols the next day near Samaria. But his account of your adventure, on the ground precisely where it occurred, modest as it was, gave me a more thrilling idea of your danger, and of his noble interposition, than any previous descriptions had given. It was characteristic of him. He was impetuous in his feelings and actions, frank, faithful and noble.

"This journey to Mosul he had in mind when we were at Damascus. M. and myself intended to go on from Damascus, across the country, but the state of the interior forbade a lady to attempt this, and we reluctantly abandoned it. Still we talked with him of accompanying him this winter, a plan that was forbidden by our sad call to return to America. When we read his letter last week in the *Observer*, describing his voyage down the Tigris, we again and again expressed our regret that we were not with him, and the very day that you sent me word of his death, M. had been saying 'Don't you wish we were with Righter on the Tigris?' I have often before me the pleasures of that journey, yet to be made, but I know no spot in all the East to which I shall direct my steps with so much of interest and grief, as to the grave of our friend. You have already printed much that has been said by those who knew him as a missionary, perhaps it will not be out of place to print these memories of him by one who knew him as a companion and friend.

"W. C. P."

From the Bible Society Record.

ON THE DEATH OF THE REV. C. N. RIGHTER.

THE PILGRIM AT REST.

AND he is gone, the young, the noble hearted,
Who tenderest ties for his Redeemer burst,
And strong in faith, the Word of Life imparted
To those who for its precious tidings thirst.

Yes, God *was* good;* for by his mercy cherished,
He walked unhurt, where countless thousands bled;
And where his suffering fellow-creatures perished,
The "strong right hand" his steps in safety led.

Beside the bed where dying ones in anguish
Appealed for aid to light them on their way,
And where the weary in their sadness languish,
He stood, "a gentle presence," day by day.

I see the failing eye his face exploring,
Which, like an angel's, beams with lucid light;
I hear his voice, God's precious words outpouring
And holding Christ before the sinner's sight.

Not the mere form, oh, not the sculptured image;
Not the carved ivory, nor the senseless wood;
Not the racked form, the marred and blood-stained visage,
With pierced hands extended on the rood!

* Mr. Righter "especially dwelt on the goodness of God: 'How good God is: O how good He is.'"—MR. WALKER.

Not this, but as a God of rich compassion,
The trembling sinner waiting to forgive;
Ready to wash him from each past transgression,
Receive him to His arms, and bid him live.

How many an eye, the mists of death o'erfilming,
Has brightened at thy words of gentle power!
How many a heart has opened glad and willing,
As to the rain, the parched and dying flower!

Glorious thy mission in that field of sadness,
And well fulfilled, until thou journeyed on,
With constant heart, upborne in Christian gladness,
To other lands, by Christ already won.

And as in devious ways thy feet were turning,
The Book of God still scattering by the way,
How brightly in thy heart His love was burning,
A fire by night, a sheltering cloud by day.

God was with thee, when o'er the current slowly
Floated thy raft, borne on with praise to Him;
He never left thee, pilgrim pure and holy,
In morning sunshine, or when day grew dim.

God was with thee! and when amid the mountains,
And in the glens, gleamed forth His power divine,
He gave thee there to quaff the living fountains,
Sweeter and purer than earth's costliest wine.

His goodness led thee till thy feet had entered
The little "Tadmor" where his children dwell,
And gave thee rest where his dear Church has centred,
Within the music of the Sabbath bell.

And then He called thee—oh, that voice so thrilling,
All that it said we cannot learn below;
But that with triumph all thy heart was filling,
Thy broken words have taught us well to know.

Oh, what a Sabbath of intense communion
Was that which God bestowed upon his child!
And, with his Saviour what a perfect union!
Oh, with what brightness the Deliverer smiled!

God's glory there was round about him shining,
His holy presence all the place imbued,
More and yet more the dying saint refining,
While round him crowds of weeping brethren stood.

As o'er her darling's couch a mother bending,
Lest fright or pain should make the loved one weep,
So by *his* couch his Saviour was attending,
Until He gave "to his beloved sleep."

Yes, thus He comes, and with his sweet caressing,
Soothes the dear child that He had died to save;
Lays hands upon him richly filled with blessing;
And guards his ashes in a foreign grave.

H. A. L.

February, 1857

THE END.

www.ingramcontent.com/pod-product-compliance
Lightning Source LLC
LaVergne TN
LVHW020212110826
845151LV00003B/692

* 9 7 8 1 4 2 5 5 3 4 7 5 2 *